God's Word tells us, "Happy is the person who finds wisdom and gains understanding" (Proverbs 3:13, NLT). *To Fly Again* is full of godly wisdom, provided by a woman who has been to the edge and back, who has stared death in the face, who has experienced tragic loss, and who has experienced the very worst and best of human nature. Gracia Burnham speaks with authority gained from her dramatic real-life experiences and from clear confirmations of God's amazing grace.

VONETTE BRIGHT
Cofounder, Campus Crusade for Christ International

In *To Fly Again*, Gracia Burnham draws from a deep well of insight, understanding, and experience. Through her writing and by her life, she shows all of us who have had our hearts broken by sorrow and our wings clipped by disappointment and difficulty what it looks like to take flight toward a joyful future, full of faith, despite our losses.

NANCY GUTHRIE
Author, *Holding On to Hope*

To Fly Again is a down-to-earth analysis of some of life's most haunting questions. It dispels the myth of the super-missionary, leaving the reader something better in return—a confidence that any Christian, no matter how weak, can be victorious in the midst of great trials.

KEN HORN
Managing Editor, *Today's Pentecostal Evangel*

In *To Fly Again*, there are more practical lessons about living in the wake of unexplainable tragedy than in any book of our time. If you're facing personal heartbreak, you'll think Gracia Burnham has been reading your diary.

DR. WOODROW KROLL
President and Bible teacher, Back to the Bible International

During their ordeal as hostages of the Abu Sayyaf, Martin and Gracia Burnham lived these words: "Greater love hath no man than this, that a man lay down his life for his friends." As you read this book, you too will be inspired to serve others, even during difficult times.

ROSS PEROT

Challenging! Like Christ's parables, Gracia's stories teach. With humor, suspense, utter frankness, and spiritual insight, Gracia faces her own foibles and failures. Scripture principles flow naturally without being "preachy." Gracia provoked me to examine myself, acknowledge weaknesses, and appreciate God's sovereign grace.

WENTWORTH PIKE
Missionary emeritus, Action International Ministries

Gracia Burnham has lived life and suffered much. She models how to respond to our circumstances and illustrates how our faith results in growth. Gracia is *no* theoretician—she has weathered the storms and traveled down dark valleys. It is a person like her who can instruct us with integrity, grace, and humility. This book is a must read for anyone who is in the midst of the refiner's fire.

DENNIS RAINEY
President, FamilyLife

Gracia Burnham offers no pat answers to the problem of pain, just incredible insights into the heart of a God who never turns a deaf ear to our cries for help and never wastes our experiences. No matter your situation, you will find renewed hope in *To Fly Again*.

DR. ROBERT H. SCHULLER
Founder, Crystal Cathedral

Gracia Burnham demonstrates with her life and witness that hope is not a desire for a positive outcome. Hope is not an emotion that causes us to feel upbeat. Even before the tragedy of being held hostage by Muslim terrorists and witnessing the death of her husband, Gracia did not hope that life on earth would be perfect. For Gracia, Hope is a person—Jesus Christ. Those of us who have had the honor of spending a little time with her have been touched by the strength of her character—His character.

TOM WHITE
Director, The Voice of the Martyrs

TO Fly AGAIN

GRACIA BURNHAM
WITH DEAN MERRILL

TYNDALE HOUSE PUBLISHERS, INC.
WHEATON, ILLINOIS

Visit Tyndale's exciting Web site at www.tyndale.com

TYNDALE is a registered trademark of Tyndale House Publishers, Inc.

Tyndale's quill logo is a trademark of Tyndale House Publishers, Inc.

To Fly Again

Designed by Beth Sparkman

Library of Congress Cataloging-in-Publication Data

Burnham, Gracia.
    To fly again : surviving the tailspins of life / Gracia Burnham, with Dean Merrill.
    p. cm.
    Includes bibliographical references.
    ISBN 1-4143-0123-5 (hc) — ISBN 1-4143-0125-1 (sc)
    1. Consolation. 2. Burnham, Gracia. I. Merrill, Dean. II. Title.
BV4905.3.B87 2005
248.8'6—dc22   2004020161

Printed in the United States of America

09   08   07   06   05
5   4   3   2   1

Contents

The apostle Paul, A.D. 55:

I think you ought to know, dear brothers and sisters, about the trouble we went through in the province of Asia. We were crushed and completely overwhelmed, and we thought we would never live through it. In fact, we expected to die. But as a result, we learned not to rely on ourselves, but on God who can raise the dead. And he did deliver us from mortal danger. And we are confident that he will continue to deliver us. He will rescue us because you are helping by praying for us. As a result, many will give thanks to God because so many people's prayers for our safety have been answered.

2 Corinthians 1:8-11

Preface

Ross Perot has helped many who find themselves in need. Having followed news of the Burnhams' captivity and Gracia's return to America, Ross Perot stepped in to offer Gracia and her children help and support. The Burnhams view him as one of their heroes.

Missionaries Martin and Gracia Burnham dedicated their lives to helping others. For over fifteen years, they lived and served among the poor on the Philippine islands of Luzon and Mindanao. But their work was interrupted in May 2001 when they were captured and held hostage for over a year by members of the Abu Sayyaf terrorist group.

The U.S. government worked diligently to rescue the Burnhams, finally sending a military team into the jungle to advise Philippine government troops. On June 7, 2002, after a year of pursuit, Philippine soldiers surprised the kidnappers and launched a rescue attempt. Gracia was rescued but Martin was killed in a gun battle between the kidnappers and the soldiers.

During their hostage ordeal, the Burnhams lived by these words:

GREATER LOVE HATH NO MAN THAN THIS,
THAT A MAN LAY DOWN HIS LIFE FOR HIS
FRIENDS.

Throughout their missionary careers, they had been
inspired by these words from Isaiah:

WHO WILL GO? SEND ME.

As you read this book, you too will be inspired to
serve others, even during difficult times.

Ross Perot

Introduction

There's something slightly odd about me writing a book on handling upheaval in your life—when my life still isn't all that well put together. Whenever I go out to speak these days, I cringe when people come up afterward and gush, "I admire you so much! You are such a special person!" I want to look behind me and see whom they could possibly be talking about.

One day after I'd gotten all dressed up for a speaking engagement—you know, heels and everything—I headed to the van and reached for the door handle. Peering inside . . . I thought a bomb had gone off. Trash was everywhere. I decided it wouldn't do for Mrs. Featured Speaker to show up in such a messy vehicle.

I grabbed a box from the garage and began throwing stuff into it: empty McDonald's cups, a plate and fork with dried food on it, one of the kids' change of clothes, even some crayons (my kids are long past the crayon age—what were *those* doing in there?!). I would have used the minivac on the floor to get the rest of the dirt only I knew I couldn't find it in the messy garage, and I was out of time anyway.

So I just drove away and made it to the church on

time, where I was greeted with warm words of admiration. If they only knew.

But here and there along the way over the past year or two, I've gleaned some fresh understanding of what's really important in life, and what is secondary. I've had time to reflect on the meaning of my jungle ordeal, and how it applies to the stresses other people are going through. God has been teaching me some perspectives that perhaps make this book worthwhile after all.

A lot of his teaching seems to come while I'm driving—which can be dangerous. It's about the only time I can sit still and concentrate for an extended period. I often have to pull over into a parking lot or a gas station to write for a while.

Sometimes when I get home and look at the notes I've scribbled, they make no sense. But other times, they spark more ideas, and some are included in this book.

One night, my oldest son, Jeff, simply *had* to get to an auto repair shop before it closed. I had just arrived home and was getting a bowl of chili for myself.

"Can I just eat this chili first?" I asked him.

"No, no, Mom—we gotta go!" he urged. "You follow me, so you can bring me back after I drop my car off."

I trudged out to the van and began following him down the road, chili bowl in one hand. All of a sudden, I had this great thought for the book!

In that moment, I realized something. *Gracia, you cannot keep following Jeff while eating a bowl of chili and recording your thoughts at the same time. You're just going to have to let the thought go.*

So that's what happened. I never got to write down my brainstorm, and it's lost forever. The world will never know how brilliant it was!

But other thoughts have been captured. As you read this book, I hope you don't think I'm preaching at you, or that I have it all together. I'll be the first to tell you that I don't. And my kids would second that. I'm just a person with a unique story whom the Lord has graced over and over again.

God knows all about the crosswinds that batter our lives—yours and mine—tossing us, like a fragile aircraft, into a tailspin. He calmly guides our shaky hands on the stick, showing us how to level out again and keep flying safely. We won't crash after all.

I started this book with fear and trembling. As I wrote, it helped me. Maybe it will help you, too.

1

Unfinished Lists

I found an old list of mine the other day—the unfinished one I left on the little desk beside the kitchen counter of our home in the Philippines when I left that fateful day to meet my husband in Manila. I expected to whisk Martin away for an anniversary weekend by the sea and return home a few days later. As the world now knows, we never got back to that home. We spent the next year in the ruthless hands of the Abu Sayyaf, a Muslim terrorist group that demanded one million dollars for our release. Martin, my husband, came back to America in a casket. I returned in a wheelchair with a bullet hole through my right leg.

Months later, a dear couple who had come to Martin's funeral kindly volunteered to pack up our belongings in that home in Aritao and ship them to me. When the truck rolled up to our house in Rose Hill, Kansas, where I had begun rebuilding my life with our three growing children, I watched the crates come off the back. Eventually, amid clothes and files and Martin's tools and beloved photos of happy days, I came across my steno pad. The list from May 2001 said:

- *Do end-of-month bookkeeping.*
- *Move furniture in the guesthouse.*
- *Move our mattresses back here.* (We had loaned some of our bedding to the mission guesthouse, which was having a large crowd just then.)
- *Service the radio battery.*
- *Order name tags for Jeff's clothing.* (Our son needed them for boarding school.)
- *Fix up the computer table in the library.*
- *Mike Fulford says SIL/Wycliffe owes us 191 gallons of avgas. Resolve this.* (Avgas is fuel for airplanes.)
- *Do next week's menu.*
- *Put Martin's toolbox away.*
- *Pay the helpers.*

How busy I was! How productive! I was a take-charge, get-it-done missionary wife and mom. Of the many small joys in life, few compared with the quiet pleasure of marking something off my to-do list. The fact that eight or ten or a dozen other items still awaited my attention did not diminish the reward of telling myself, *Well, at least I got that one done.*

I heard about one man who, in making his lists, would add a few tasks he had already taken care of—just so when he got to the end of the paper, he could go back and strike them out again. Psychologically, it felt good to tell himself he had already accomplished a few things. Now the rest of the list did not seem so daunting.

Lists supervise our lives, it seems, whether jotted in Day-Timers, on yellow stickees, on pastel notepads made

4

especially for the purpose, on the back of grocery store checkout tapes—or only on the front wall of our minds. A mother's work is never done, says the old proverb. And instinctively we know, whether we are parents or not, that if we don't itemize the specific tasks somewhere, the work will get totally out of hand. That was why I tried to keep my steno pad close at hand: I wanted to stay on top of everything.

And then—in a moment of time—everything changed. I became a hostage who had lost all control of my life, my schedule, and my future. I could only sit on the ground and stare at the jungle, wondering what would come next. Did the unfinished items on that list back in the kitchen ever get done? I had no way to find out. In fact, to this day I still don't know. My world had forever shifted.

Since my return to the States, I've met many other people whose world has been rocked unexpectedly. I spoke not long ago to a support group of cancer victims, survivors, and caregivers. The invitation had come for a date just a few weeks before Christmas, and I wasn't sure I should accept in light of preholiday busyness. But in the end, I said yes and afterward was glad I did.

I arrived that morning to find some two hundred people gathered in an upstairs hall. As I waited in the front row, an attractive young woman came up to me. She introduced herself and pointed out her husband, whose hair was now gone because of chemotherapy.

"You know, this has been a really tough time for us," she said. "We have three little kids. But the Lord has been faithful to help us so far. We're looking forward to your message of hope."

I took her hand and told her I appreciated her making the effort to come. Soon it was time for me to stand up and begin my talk.

"As you know, I stand before you today as a survivor of sorts," I began. "My battle was not against cancer, of course, but against the schemes of a group of killers in the Philippine jungle." I went on to recount how it all broke loose for Martin and me: the trip to the Dos Palmas Resort, the romantic evening, the sudden banging on the door early the next morning, the scramble for my clothes, the gun barrel in my back as I was prodded down the catwalk to the waiting speedboat, the boat's escape onto open water, and my whisper to Martin just then: "We are in big trouble."

I paused and looked across the room of somber faces. "In that one moment, I lost all control of my life. I would be told from that point onward where to sleep, how to dress, what to eat (if at all), even where to go to the bathroom. If I didn't like the options, which I often didn't, that was just too bad. My existence was out of my hands."

The audience quickly began to identify with my predicament, it seemed. They, too, had been going along living a normal life, or so they thought, until the fateful day in a doctor's office somewhere when the person in a white coat said, "Your lab results came back, and I'm sorry to tell you that you have a malignancy." In that moment, everything changed. The patients took in a breath of air and couldn't push it out again. They sat transfixed, staring at the physician, fumbling for words. Surely it wasn't true. Yes, it was—this was not a joke. The foundation of their life quivered as in an earthquake, threatening to crack.

As I continued to speak, I noticed people nodding their heads. The Kleenexes came out in greater numbers than usual. I began realizing that I had more in common with this audience than I had expected.

"How do we manage when life spins out of control in a single day?" I said. "What do we do when all our plans and goals are put on hold, when everything we had intended to do and see and accomplish gets swept aside, and we don't know if we'll ever get back to familiar ground? How do we keep our sanity? How do we avoid slipping into a personal canyon of despair?

"I remember a particularly frightening Thursday morning in the jungle, the day of Gun Battle Number 13. We endured seventeen of these altogether, where our little group would be spotted by the Philippine military, who were trying to rescue us hostages but were ill-trained to do so. While their intentions were good, their technique was altogether dangerous, not only for the terrorists but for us as well.

"On this day Martin and I had just built a small fire to heat water for a cup of tea. Our recently washed clothes were strewn out on bushes to dry in the sun.

Suddenly, gunfire erupted. We had to get out of that place immediately.

"Normally, we tried to keep our belongings fairly well consolidated for such emergencies. But in this moment, our stuff was everywhere. We were totally unprepared.

"We instantly hit the ground, of course. As bullets continued to whiz past our heads, Martin gingerly reached up to pull the cord that tied one end of our hammock to a tree. He then scooted along the ground to do the same to the opposite cord. We squashed the hammock into our backpack and then dashed for cover, abandoning nearly everything else—extra clothes, cooking utensils, my hairbrush, and other necessities.

"Soon we found ourselves wading through a swamp that came up to our waists. We emerged on the other side and flopped down to rest. I looked at my husband with total exhaustion.

"In that desperate hour, my wonderful husband said, 'Gracia, let's remind ourselves of what we know is true.' We had no Bible to consult; we could lean only on what we had stored in our memories. From that reserve, we began to recite: 'If God be for us, who can be against us?' (Romans 8:31, KJV).

"One of us said, 'Where does it say in Scripture, "I have loved thee with an everlasting love"?' (It's in the Old Testament, Jeremiah 31:3, KJV.)

" 'And then what about that part at the beginning of Ephesians: "Blessed be the God and Father of our Lord Jesus Christ, who hath blessed us with all spiritual blessings in heavenly places in Christ"?' (Ephesians 1:3, KJV).

"We went on sharing Scriptures such as these, trying to anchor ourselves in the truth we could trust, the truth that God is with us through the tunnel, through the valley, through the gun battle. He stands with us through the medical prognosis that terrorizes us, through every horrible thing that life throws our way. We don't go through these things alone. We walk with our hands in the hand of the One who turns night into day.

"Ladies and gentlemen, a bad thing happened to me—and to you, too. We didn't ask for any of this; we didn't deserve it. But it came upon us regardless. The way of wisdom in going forward, I believe, is to keep walking with Jesus. He knows the road when we don't."

At the end of my forty-minute talk, the meeting ended, and I moved over to a table to greet people and sign copies of my book, *In the Presence of My Enemies*. The line moved slowly that day, as each person seemed to have a story to tell.

"I'm a caregiver for my mother, who was too sick to come today. . . ."

"I'm a cancer survivor; I've been cancer-free for five years. . . ." I began to notice that each person who had beaten the disease wanted to tell me the time length of their victory.

"Thanks for the neat message of hope. . . ."

One lady gave me a gift of some lovely china that she had painted by hand.

But the words that stuck most vividly in my mind came from several people who said, "I wouldn't trade my cancer experience for anything, because it has brought me closer to God" or ". . . because it has thrown me onto the Lord."

I was shocked. Were they serious? Could anyone actually view cancer as a good thing?

Apparently so. The day that had devastated their life turned out to be the beginning of their spiritual rebirth. They had found new hope and new life in Jesus Christ.

It is not easy to come to this perspective, I admit. Sometimes the discomfort overwhelms us temporarily. We can't see straight or think straight because we are so miserable.

Once as we were wandering in the jungle, the Abu Sayyaf picked out a campsite on a cliff that overlooked a beautiful river. It was close to a village, but we had to stay away from civilization as much as possible to avoid discovery. So we settled there instead for about ten days. The cliff had trees from which the group's hammocks could be hung.

Martin and I didn't yet have a hammock, however; we were still sleeping on the ground. And the slope of the cliff was too steep for sleeping.

Hurayra, our assigned guard, took it upon himself to dig a little flat spot, like a shelf, into the side of the cliff. It was about six feet long and wide enough for the two of us to lie down inside it.

The worst part, however, were the swarms of flies that inhabited this cliff. They buzzed around everyone's head incessantly. With nothing to do, Martin and I would sit and talk, swatting flies away almost constantly. It got so bad that after a while, we would seek protection by crawling under our *malongs*, the long Filipino piece of fabric that serves as everything from a towel to a skirt to a knapsack.

This kept the flies away—but it was also very hot. The sun would beat down until we were about to suffocate. We would eventually have to sit up to get some fresh air, fanning ourselves and flailing at the flies again until we were exhausted. The *malong* had to be better than this, we would think. And so the cycle would begin all over.

I began to grow very depressed. "I really miss my mom," I said to Martin one day. "I just need her to be here and hold my hand." I began to cry. My mother, with her warm and soothing accent from southern "Missourah" where she grew up, could calm her little girl's nerves and somehow make it all better, I just knew.

I lay down under the *malong* again and started sobbing. Martin reached over to pat my shoulder, but there was nothing further he could do for me. The Abu Sayyaf members heard me carrying on, I'm sure, and even though they were tough warriors, they seemed to feel sorry for me. Just not sorry enough to release us.

We eventually left that cliffside to move on to another place, and another, and then another. I had to come, in time, to the understanding that while my wonderful mother was ten time zones away, someone even greater and more capable to sustain and comfort me was nearby: the Lord himself. He saw my weariness,

my frustration, my lack of hope, and in his own ways he
was there to lift me and encourage me.

The times when life seems unmanageable to us are the
times when we find out that God is truly good. His goodness is shown not just in blessing us with material
comforts: houses, cars, television sets, vacations. His
goodness shines through in the times when we are
uncomfortable, when all of life seems to have gone crazy.

One of the psalms we were able to recall, and even
write down, in the jungle was the uplifting Psalm 100,
including the line "Serve the LORD with gladness" (verse
2, KJV), which was Martin's motto and watchword. There
is another gem in the last verse of the same psalm that says:

For the LORD is good and his love endures forever;
his faithfulness continues through all generations.

(verse 5, NIV)

"The Lord is good." That simple truth can sustain us
through dreadful circumstances.

I would have to tell you that the various gods of the
tribal people whom we served in the Philippines were
not what you could call "good." Their supposed rules and
proclamations often worked to the detriment of the
villagers. We would see children withering away without
proper nourishment, even though the jungle held an
abundant supply of nutritious tropical fruits. "No, you
are not allowed to eat that fruit," said the witch doctor.
"It is forbidden." And so, the obedient parents would
conform to what their gods announced, even if it led to

burying a beloved child who eventually had starved to death.

In contrast, the Lord God is fundamentally good-hearted, loving, and concerned for his children of all ages. We must never forget that. He has a thousand ways to sustain us through our darkest hours. Life sometimes throws us vicious surprises—but he is not surprised. He stands ready to shower us with his love that "endures forever . . . through all generations."

The poet J. J. Lynch wrote:

> *Say not, my soul, "From whence*
> *Can God relieve my care?"*
> *Remember that Omnipotence*
> *Hath servants everywhere.*[1]

I think of that whenever God sends someone to help me, a widow and single mother, these days. Whenever someone shows me how to reprogram my home's security code or sends me an encouraging card or gives me a song to lift my spirit, I say to myself, *Ah, yes—Omnipotence hath servants everywhere.* I never know when one of these is going to show up, and neither do you.

There are things we can do in the midst of our trial to make it less burdensome, more manageable. As we learn to work with the God who loves us rather than work against him, we can lessen our pain.

To these things we turn our attention in the coming chapters.

2

*The Guarantee
Nobody Wants*

If you could put the history of your life onto a computer screen, highlight just one day, and then punch *Delete*, which day would you choose? Is there a certain twenty-four-hour period that you wish had never happened?

Some people would point to the Saturday night of a car accident. Some, like my friends at the cancer support center, would say a certain doctor's appointment. Others, tragically, might select their wedding day. For me, obviously, it would be May 27, 2001—the Sunday that Martin and I were captured.

If only . . .

While we fantasize about what life might have been like without our difficult junctures, the truth is that these intersections are not abnormal. Jesus told his disciples at the close of their final Passover evening together: "Here on earth you will have many trials and sorrows" (John 16:33). He didn't say "may" or "might" or "could" or "possibly" or any other tentative word. He said, flat out, you *will* have trouble. Guaranteed. It's going to happen.

Yes, he followed immediately with a brighter encouragement: "But take heart, because I have overcome the world." I will talk a bit later about what that means. But for now, let us accept the reality that bad things are going to happen to us, if they haven't already.

I didn't really understand that for the first forty-two years of my life. I was born into a loving family, had lots of friends growing up, became a believer in the Lord Jesus at an early age, was popular in high school and college, and finally married a terrific guy who had an incredible gift of piloting airplanes. Martin was no ordinary flyboy. He could put a loaded Cessna down on the exact spot he wanted in a small jungle clearing and get the plane stopped in the next few hundred feet. People were amazed at his talent.

Plus, he loved people. That's what made him want to use his piloting skills to make a difference in this world.

So we packed up and left the American dream to go to a distant country where Martin flew food, medicine, fuel for generators, and other cargo—including people—into some of the most primitive places in the world. Missionary families were living in remote villages, learning obscure languages, and telling poor tribal people that they didn't have to keep sacrificing their livestock to the spirits of their dead ancestors. Instead, a loving God had made a way to rescue them from their sin and unhappiness. He had sent his perfect Son, Jesus, to pay the penalty for all our sins, so we could have a relationship with a holy God.

And Martin's role in getting that message across was to fly.

Meanwhile, what was my role? What talents had God given me?

Well, I do like to talk! That's about it. Oh—and I can make a halfway decent pizza.

So God took what I had and put it to use. I became the radio operator for our mission, where I could sit at a small table with a microphone and do a lot of talking. I called every missionary in the jungle twice a day to take their grocery orders, relay messages to town, schedule flights, and just encourage them. It was great. And when the missionaries would come to our center for a break, I made sure they had a comfortable bed to sleep in, plus an invitation to come over to our place that evening for a movie and . . . pizza, of course.

We did this for sixteen years and loved it. We had three children along the way. They grew up loving the Philippines as much as we did.

Then came the day when Martin needed to go to another island to fill in for a pilot whose father had died back in the States. I opted to go with him, and as a special treat, I arranged for us to celebrate our anniversary with just twenty-four hours at Dos Palmas. The rest of the story, you already know.

That was the point where my "easy" life changed. I guess I shouldn't have been surprised, if I had taken John 16:33 seriously. But I had not. I thought the Burnham family was on a roll that would last our entire lives. I hadn't paid attention to the guarantee.

The truth is, trials and trouble and tribulation come to us all. Perhaps you've felt the pain of being misunderstood by family members or the ache of depression. Maybe you've had to face the loss of a job, or the realization that you're unloved, or not as attractive in the social marketplace as other people with better-looking bodies, silkier hair, more perfect teeth. Perhaps you've been treated unfairly, or been rejected for no valid reason. Every one of these can be as much a problem as being held at gunpoint by terrorists. Everyone's trial is unique and real.

And the stress goes on and on, with no end in sight. I read somewhere that Noah and his family endured 377 days on the ark during the great Flood: If you add up all the time they waited for the rain to start, the actual 40 days and nights of downpour, and the long period during which the water receded and the ground dried enough for them to disembark, the number comes to 377. That struck me, because that is almost precisely how long Martin and I were in captivity.

I wonder if Mrs. Noah ever said to her husband, "Are we ever going to get out of here? The stench is overwhelming me. We're going to be stuck on this boat with these animals forever."

When windstorms came along and rocked them until they were seasick, did they fear for their life? What did Noah say then?

If you carefully read the Lord's instructions to Noah in Genesis 6 and 7, you'll discover that God talks a lot about *going into* the ark to avoid drowning. He says nothing about Noah and his family eventually *getting out* of the ark. Perhaps that was implied; I can't say. Did they worry that they might be floating forever? What if their food for the animals ran out? What if they themselves eventually ran out of food? What then?

"Here on earth you will have many trials and sorrows," said Jesus—but then he continued with the offsetting advice to "take heart, because I have overcome the world." In the midst of our trouble, there is a good thing: He has conquered all.

Many Christians read this verse and come to a false conclusion: They expect Jesus to shield them from the world's abundance of trials. They think, perhaps wistfully, that the second part of the verse negates the first half. My experience tells me that this is not true.

In fact, it wasn't true even for Jesus himself. He made this statement, then promptly stood up, walked out the door into the nighttime air, and headed for the Cross. Less than fifteen hours later, he was bleeding profusely and gasping for breath on a Roman torture apparatus. This was "overcoming the world"? How so?

What he meant was that by his death, he would overcome the curse of sin, death, and hell. He would put in motion the means of redemption for us all. His sacrifice would be enough to free us from eternal condemnation. His ultimate victory over Satan would be assured.

Even before that takes place at the end of time, the promise of Jesus that night long ago means two things to us:

1. He will go *through* our trials alongside us.
2. We will go to heaven to be with him when we die.

As a result, we are never alone. So often as I lay on the jungle floor at night unsuccessfully trying to get comfortable enough to sleep, I felt alone. I was stinky and dirty; there was no place to take a bath; my hair was a disaster; I had no clean clothes to put on the next morning; I felt more like an animal than a human being. But I was never alone. Christ was right there with me.

In John 14:27 Jesus told his disciples, "I am leaving you with a gift—peace of mind and heart. And the peace I give isn't like the peace the world gives. So don't be troubled or afraid."

The end result of his presence in our lives is a deep and lasting peace. Unlike worldly peace, which is usually defined only as the absence of conflict, this peace is confident assurance in any circumstance. Another Scripture speaks about how to "experience God's peace, which is far more wonderful than the human mind can understand. His peace will guard your hearts and minds as you live in Christ Jesus" (Philippians 4:7).

The trouble is guaranteed. But so is the peace.

The apostle Paul, whom the whole Christian world reveres as a huge success, once made a list of all the things that had gone wrong during his ministry. He included it in his second letter to the Corinthian church, chapter 11, verses 24-33:

- Five beatings with a lash
- Three beatings with a rod
- One bludgeoning with stones until he blacked out
- Three shipwrecks
- Twenty-four hours in open water trying to stay afloat
- Having to cross flooded rivers
- Being chased by various bandits
- Being undermined by "false brothers"
- Lack of sleep
- Hunger and thirst
- Inadequate clothing in the cold
- Immature and eccentric churches to oversee
- Having to run for his life from the arresting authorities

And we call this man a great apostle! We blithely read his hair-raising episodes and hail him as a wonderful first-century church leader.

If he were with us today, he would affirm what Jesus said in John 15:20-21, "Do you remember what I told you? 'A servant is not greater than the master.' Since they persecuted me, naturally they will persecute you. And if they had listened to me, they would listen to you! The people of the world will hate you because you belong to me, for they don't know God who sent me."

This prediction applies not only to Paul's time but to ours as well. Christians learn to persevere in the midst of problems, not in their absence.

I saw a poster at church one Sunday advertising that the chorale from Calvary Bible College, my alma mater, would be coming to a nearby church soon. I had sung in that choir long ago; in fact, it was the excellence of their music that first drew me, as a high school student, to want to attend that college.

They would be singing on a Sunday night. My kids and I decided to skip the evening church service we normally attended and drove an hour or so up the road to hear the choir. As we entered the church, I was pleased to see some old friends who had stayed attached to the college as I had. We greeted each other and then soon found a place to sit near the front, on the right side.

The forty or so singers filed onto the risers and began their concert. The quality was excellent. I was thoroughly enjoying it, and so were my kids.

In time they came to the familiar spiritual "Didn't My Lord Deliver Daniel?" I noticed people's shoulders bobbing along to the tune and rhythm—until all of a sudden, I zeroed in on the lyrics:

> *"Didn't my Lord deliver Daniel?*
> *Then why not ev-e-ry man?"*

I froze in my seat. *Yeah—why not?* I thought. God delivered Daniel from the lion's den. Why didn't he deliver Martin from the jungle terrorists?

The original lyrics were no doubt meant as an uplifting encouragement: *In light of the great things God did for*

Daniel, look what he can do for you. But for me, the words raised a perplexing dilemma.

For the next three songs or so, I didn't hear a note. I was too consumed with processing this question in my mind. There in the pew, I opened my Bible to Hebrews 11 and began to read:

> *By faith these people overthrew kingdoms, ruled with justice, and received what God had promised them. They shut the mouths of lions, quenched the flames of fire, and escaped death by the edge of the sword. Their weakness was turned to strength. They became strong in battle and put whole armies to flight. Women received their loved ones back again from death. (verses 33-35a)*

I caught my breath at that last sentence. Wouldn't that have been a wonderful reversal for our family? However, it had not happened. I kept reading:

> *But others trusted God and were tortured, preferring to die rather than turn from God and be free. They placed their hope in the resurrection to a better life. Some were mocked, and their backs were cut open with whips. Others were chained in dungeons. Some died by stoning, and some were sawed in half; others were killed with the sword. Some went about in skins of sheep and goats, hungry and oppressed and mistreated. They were too good for this world. They wandered over deserts and mountains, hiding in caves and holes in the ground.*

25

All of these people we have mentioned received God's approval because of their faith, yet none of them received all that God had promised. For God had far better things in mind for us that would also benefit them, for they can't receive the prize at the end of the race until we finish the race. (verses 35b-40)

Soon I was jotting notes in my notebook, while the concert rolled on. At least Martin didn't die horribly, in one of the ways mentioned in the passage. He was shot in the chest and quickly lost consciousness as his blood pressure plummeted. He certainly wasn't tortured or taunted with a demand to renounce Christ. I was grateful for that much.

People today call Martin a martyr for Christ, and I'm never quite sure what to think about that. Neither he nor I was targeted *because* we were Christians; we just happened to be in the wrong place at the wrong time as a band of kidnappers were rounding up their bargaining chips. Meanwhile, all over the world, other Christians in our time are being hounded, harassed, and killed for their faith.

Even so, the loss of Martin was a huge sorrow for me. It certainly fulfilled the pledge that difficulty would come my way. And yet, as the Scripture says, "God had far better things in mind for us." He is sovereign. He can choose the ending of a person's life as he sees fit. And he can be glorified in any number of ways.

I closed my Bible and notebook to resume listening to the concert. As I drove my kids home that night, I wasn't quite as talkative as I had been on the way to the church. I was thinking about the fact that the peacefulness and security we currently enjoy is not promised forever. But whatever the future brings, the Christ who went to the Cross will be with us to sustain and to redeem. As Hebrews 13 reminds us:

> God has said,
>
> "I will never fail you.
>   I will never forsake you."
>
> That is why we can say with confidence,
>
> "The Lord is my helper,
>   so I will not be afraid.
>   What can mere mortals do to me?" (verses 5-6)

3

What
Defines You?

I was coming home from Wichita late one morning and stopped for a red light at the intersection of Kellogg and Andover roads. A woman in her midthirties rolled up beside me in a silver-colored car.

Out of the corner of my eye I noticed that she was talking on a cell phone. Her wrist jewelry was beautiful; her dark hair looked great; her outfit was "power red." Clearly a working professional, she was the picture of poise and competence. I thought, *She's on her way somewhere to do something really important.*

The light changed, and she headed on straight as I turned. For some reason, I kept thinking about her as I drove south the seven miles to my home. I wondered if she was happy. I wondered if she had kids somewhere, in school or in day care. I wondered if the morning routine at her house had been smooth or harried.

Then an odd thought crossed my mind. *What if her cell phone were taken away?*

She wouldn't be able to communicate on the road. Her ability to "network" would be severely hampered.

What if she didn't have that nice car?

She would have a much harder time keeping her

appointments. In fact, she might find it impossible to do her present work and have to change jobs.

What if her wardrobe was old and plain, instead of up-to-date and fresh? She wouldn't make such a positive impression on clients.

I wasn't meaning to criticize her in any way. In one sense, I actually admired her. I was just musing about the things that support us in our choices. Who would she be without them?

Who are any of us down deep inside, minus the accessories of modern life? If some force vacuumed away our many possessions, what would be left?

One tribe in the Philippines has a unique way of defining people. The first time Martin flew into their village, the resident missionary began to introduce him to the people. He knew Martin's name, obviously, but in keeping with the local culture, he said in front of the crowd, "Now, you have a son, is that correct?"

"Yes," Martin replied.

"What is his name?"

"My oldest son is Jeffrey."

"Ah yes. So you are Inay-Jeffrey," he pronounced. The name meant "father of Jeffrey," except that Filipinos have a way of turning the *ff* sound into *p*, so it came out more like "Inay-Jappery."

That became his official name whenever he flew to this village. Nobody ever called him Martin or Mr. Burnham. His whole identity was based upon his firstborn.

The Muslims who held us captive, we learned, had a similar obsession with male offspring. Musab, a gruff leader within the Abu Sayyaf, especially wanted to sire as many sons as possible. Not to have a son was considered a disgrace.

Solaiman, the captor who related most directly to us in the early months because of his good English, was always bothered by the fact that he had no son. He thus could not properly be called Abu Solaiman, which made him inferior to the others.

Readers from other cultures will no doubt find this strange, even illogical. But is it any different from our penchant for defining ourselves by our wealth, our neighborhood, our zip code, our gold (if not platinum) credit cards, our ethnic heritage, our church affiliation, or our possessions?

Less than one-fourth of the world's population sleeps in a bed at night. Think about that for a minute. Three-fourths sleep in a hammock of some kind . . . or on a mat on a floor . . . or on a floor with no mat . . . or on the plain dirt.

Obviously, even fewer have a bedspread that matches the curtains, or a TV across the bedroom with a remote control to turn it on and off from where they recline. The belongings that matter to many of us are beyond comprehension to at least three billion other people on our planet.

I remember the day a packet arrived in the jungle camp that included a few snapshots for Martin and me. One showed my niece Sarah Tunis with a group of her college friends, who had gone on a retreat somewhere. They casually posed for the camera, and to us it was a warm reminder of "normal life" back in America.

The Abu Sayyaf, who censored everything we received, were fascinated with this photo. They eagerly passed it around, oohing and aahing as they chattered excitedly in their dialect. We wondered what was so intriguing about the picture.

Finally Martin went to inquire. In a few minutes he returned to where I was sitting on the ground.

"You'll never guess," he said.

"What?"

"They are amazed that *everybody* in the photo is wearing shoes." Not a single young person in that faraway place (wherever it was) had to go barefoot. How astounding.

When life spins out of control for us, we find out who we truly are. We may have to redefine ourselves. We may have to face the fact that our belongings and assumptions have propped us up to a precarious degree. At such times life is a matter of "just us," with no embellishments.

Jesus once reminded a man who wanted to follow him: "Foxes have dens to live in, and birds have nests, but I, the Son of Man, have no home of my own, not even a place to lay my head" (Luke 9:58). The Lord didn't seem to be particularly bothered by that; he wasn't complaining in the least. He was just stating the truth. And for him, it had no bearing on his being the "Son of Man," the chosen messenger of God almighty to the human race. He was who he was, bed or no bed, roof or no roof, money or no money.

After his resurrection, Jesus told his disciple Peter one morning beside the lakeshore, "The truth is, when you were young, you were able to do as you liked and go wherever you wanted to. But when you are old, you will stretch out your hands, and others will direct you and take you where you don't want to go" (John 21:18). No doubt that was unwelcome news for a strong, self-reliant fisherman. Peter would lose all independence, all control over his own mobility, wardrobe, and schedule.

In fact, church history tells us that Peter did indeed come to a restricted end under Roman arrest. He was crucified head downward, says tradition. Yet his place in our heart and memories is as exalted as ever.

What defines us in good times and bad is not what we have but who we are. Those who have been made sons and daughters of the King should not be measured by temporal accessories.

Earlier I noted how few people sleep in a bed at night. Just as surprising is this finding from Caslon Analytics, an Australian technology research firm: "Eighty percent of the world's population has never made a telephone call."[2] That was true of a lady who lived near us in the barrio at Aritao. She was perhaps in her seventies, with a sun-weathered face from long years of working in the rice fields.

She showed up at my door one day with her gray hair pulled back in a ponytail, her feet adorned with plastic *tsinelas* (flip-flops). "Could you help me call my daughter in Manila?" she asked shyly, explaining that an uncle had been taken to the hospital. She held out a scrap of paper with a phone number penciled on it.

"Of course I'll help you," I replied. "Come on inside." I put my arm around her shoulder as I ushered her to the telephone in our kitchen.

I dialed the number for her and then extended the receiver in her direction.

A look of horror came over her face and she began backing up. You would have thought I was pushing a snake toward her. She obviously was scared to death of this black thing in my hand with its thin cord trailing downward.

That's when it dawned on me that in all of her long life, she had never used a phone.

I didn't know enough of her language to explain very much, but I encouraged her with smiles and hand motions to take the receiver and just listen. With great trepidation she put the black thing to her ear, and then a big smile broke across her face as a familiar voice came through the line.

There was no conventional "Oh, hello" or "How are you?" or "The reason I'm calling is . . ." She just immediately plunged into the news of what was occurring in her family. As soon as she had said her piece, she handed

36

the phone back to me, thanked me profusely, and
headed out the door.

I thought, *You know, this little lady isn't stupid. She
has raised a family; she's done what she could to make life
enjoyable for the people she cares about. Just because she has
never used a phone, or eaten in a restaurant, or checked
into a hotel doesn't mean she is less of a person. She is
still a woman created in the image of God. And for that,
she has worth.*

The more we center ourselves on our true definition
in God's sight, not the possessions we have been able to
gather or the esteem that others have given us, the more
stable we will be in good times and bad. What other
people think of us—and the artificial scales on which
they rank us—is beside the point. They can make us
neither better nor worse than we already are at our core.

If we accept this reality deep inside, we will be able to
live far more peaceful lives.

4

*Anger
Doesn't Help*

I was furious.

We were on a hilltop taking a rest, and Musab—who always made me mad—was going through his backpack, trying to lighten it. Musab pretended to be the Abu Sayyaf's spiritual leader, delivering long-winded sermons on the fine points of Islam. But in reality, he was pompous and hypocritical.

As Musab pawed through his belongings that day, Martin sat nearby, a chain on his wrist. Musab carried the loose end of the chain to make double sure that Martin didn't try to escape, even though it was obvious he would never leave me behind, and the two of us weren't fast enough to outrun these young warriors, for sure.

Suddenly Musab picked up a bag of rice and swung it toward Martin. "Here—you carry this," he blurted. He could not have cared less that my husband was already hauling close to fifty pounds of gear, including M60 mortar shells that never seemed to get used.

I just fumed inside. How unfair this was. My husband was already strained to the limit, he was losing weight, and these people were systematically grinding him right into the ground.

My mental state was affected by the fact that at that time I had diarrhea, and there was no place to go in private, or means for cleaning up afterward. We could see no end to our misery. Already we'd gotten our hopes up for release a couple of times, only to be disappointed.

When the rest of the group was out of earshot, I let loose my rage. "Someday that man is going to burn in hell," I told Martin, "and I hope I'm there to see it."

Martin sighed as he looked at me through tired eyes. "Oh, Gracia," he replied, "someday that man *is* going to burn in hell if he doesn't change. But you don't want to be there to see it! Can you imagine the horror of being judged for eternity?"

No, of course not. I knew better than to revel in the thought of another human being's torment. But my emotions had gotten the better of me before Martin gently corrected me.

Later that night, we talked further. It was close to Christmas, and the guys were being rowdy. They were laughing at us and making cracks, such as, "I bet you wish you were going to be home for Christmas—." *Ha ha ha.*

Again I murmured to Martin, "Well, God will make all of this right someday. I hope that guy really suffers."

"Yes, he will," my husband replied thoughtfully. "And if anything, that should really burden our hearts for him, rather than make us happy."

I turned away and bit my lip in contemplation.

Anger in the face of trauma is understandable. But that doesn't make it productive. I found that as long as I blamed the Abu Sayyaf for our situation, my heart remained in turmoil. I blamed the terrorists; I blamed the Philippine military for their ineptness; I blamed the American government for not waving some magic wand to free us; I even blamed God because . . . well, he's in control of everything, isn't he?

Something inside us all yearns for justice and gets upset when life shows its unfair side. As Martin and I squatted around the cooking fire waiting for our portion, we would carefully watch the server pile rice on other plates but then give us only two-thirds of a cupful, solely because we were non-Filipino and non-Muslim. I wanted to scream.

Slowly I began to realize that my resentment wasn't serving any useful purpose. The alternative, of course, was to forgive, even without the benefit of an apology from the offender. I could *choose* to forgive, all by myself.

As I forgave, the anger cooled down and the hurt went away.

But then a new day would dawn, and a new injustice would erupt. I would be faced with a fresh need to forgive. Any hope in a once-for-all absolution for the Abu Sayyaf was quickly disproved. This was a conscious decision I would have to make and remake as time went by.

In fact, it became a pattern. And therein lay a path back to self-control and composure.

I did not pray, "God, help me forgive Musab." To do so would have been to dodge my own responsibility. The Lord's Prayer says that *"we* forgive those who have sinned against us" (Luke 11:4, italics added). It is not something I could pass along to a Higher, More Mellow Power. The task was squarely mine, although once I chose to obey, God certainly gave me the strength to do so.

And, of course, there is a consequence in all this. Said Jesus: "If you forgive those who sin against you, your heavenly Father will forgive you. But if you refuse to forgive others, your Father will not forgive your sins" (Matthew 6:14-15).

Now that I am back in America rearing three teen-agers, I have daily opportunity to practice what I learned in the jungle. The offenses are not nearly so heinous, of course. But my anger must still be defused. When one of my kids says something unkind to me or someone makes a wisecrack about a decision I've made, I have to remind myself that I can forgive this person just as I forgave the Abu Sayyaf.

In fact, sometimes it is a bigger struggle to forgive little things than big ones. If one of my kids forgets his assignment to take the trash out to the curb on Monday morning, I have a choice to make: Am I going to fume about this for hours, or am I going to forgive my child for being imperfect?

Obviously, I have to haul out the trash either way. But on the inside, I say, *I think I'll just forgive Zachary in my heart.* It's an act of my will.

That doesn't mean I won't mention the incident

when he gets home from school. But the tone of the words will be more constructive than accusatory.

Whenever you are hurt or wronged, your first inclination may be to lash back. Even if you thwart that urge, you may still cling to bitterness and resentment. In such a time, it's not hard to find someone who will sympathize and reinforce the anger.

You say to your friend, "You know, so-and-so really did me dirty."

And your friend replies, "Yes, they sure did, and you didn't deserve that at all. I don't blame you for being upset. I'd be mad, too."

It feels good to hear, but it only serves to churn the spirit. It doesn't help the cause of restoration.

I had been home from captivity about six months when the phone rang one day, and a man with a Filipino accent said, "Hello, my name is Captain Oliver Almonarez. I was the captain of the Scout Rangers who talked to you at the top of the hill."

I was amazed. "Oh! Yes, I remember you," I said. On the day Martin died, this was the fellow who had come over to apologize while I was waiting for the evacuation helicopter.

"I'm in Chicago visiting relatives, and I just wanted to call and wish you a merry Christmas."

"Well, that's very nice of you," I said. I waited to see what he would say next.

"After all three hostages got shot that day," he continued, "everyone was so angry with me. My superior officer yelled at me. My family, my friends, the other guys in the unit—everybody was mad at me. No one had a kind word for me. I was in a bad way.

"Then the next Monday, when you were at the Manila airport ready to fly to America, you gave your little comment to the media. You talked about your love for the Philippines, and that you were leaving a piece of your heart behind. You even thanked us in the military for trying to rescue you.

"When we all saw that you weren't angry . . . then people weren't angry with me anymore. I just wanted to thank you for what you said that day."

I replied, "Well, the Lord works in people's hearts. You're very welcome."

I had never thought about my public comments having a ripple effect in someone else's life. But, in fact, they set a new tone for what had been ugly up to that point.

A year later, Captain Almonarez called again to say he was back in Chicago for another family gathering. He really wanted to meet with me, he said. A friend of his would even drive him the seven hundred miles to Kansas!

"Oh, surely you don't want to do that," I replied. "As it so happens, I'm going to Chicago soon to speak to my book publisher's staff." We arranged to meet at Tyndale's offices.

The day came when I laid eyes again on the man whose troops had stormed the hillside that rainy afternoon, killing Martin as well as Ediborah Yap, another hostage. He walked into the room, the same broad-shouldered man about thirty years old with the handsome face and shaved head that I remembered. What he mainly wanted to tell me was that he was sorry the rescue had gone awry.

He explained his side of the story, which was that the Scout Rangers had lived in the jungle for a year and endured many hardships themselves. It certainly had not been a lark. He claimed that the American FBI had finally been able to get a cooperative courier to give Sabaya, the Abu Sayyaf's spokesperson and negotiator, a new backpack—into which they had sewn a homing device. This told the officials our general vicinity and enabled them to start tracking us.

I didn't spend a lot of time or energy trying to analyze his details, sorting out the what-ifs. I just listened to his story. It turned out the captain was a committed Christian. On the island of Iloilo where he grew up, he had become a believer at a Bible Baptist youth meeting.

When I stood up to shake his hand and say good-bye, I realized once again that forgiveness is a choice. Had his bullet possibly struck my husband? There is no way to know, and what good would it serve to know? Far better to forgive and move on.

If every time our anger flairs we choose to forgive, eventually we will find that we are not angry anymore. We are free to focus on the future with hope and peace. As Jesus put it in Luke 6:45, "A good person produces good deeds from a good heart, and an evil person produces evil deeds from an evil heart. Whatever is in your heart determines what you say." If the heart is rid of its anger, the outflow can be pure.

5

Rising above Revenge

I had been home from the Philippines just three months when September 11 rolled around—the one-year anniversary of the terrorist attacks. A citywide observance was slated that evening in the football stadium of Wichita State University. The organizers asked me to speak for about ten minutes.

What should I say on such a solemn occasion?

I chose to tell about the slow, sultry days we spent at a camp along a beautiful, rushing river, where the Abu Sayyaf told us we were relatively safe. (The camp was owned by the MILF, another group of Islamic separatist rebels.) We had plenty to eat at that point, but there was nothing to fill the days. We were bored out of our minds.

To occupy the time, we hostages told one another stories. I opted for hostage stories out of the Bible, describing people in straits similar to our own.

One was about the little girl in 2 Kings 5 who was snatched away from her home in Israel to scrub floors and peel potatoes (or whatever) in the home of Aram's commanding four-star general, Naaman. "The Bible doesn't tell either her name or her age," I said as I spoke to the Wichita crowd, "but just to make her a little more real for us, let's imagine that she was ten years old. Do we have any ten-year-olds here tonight?"

Across the bleachers, little girls waved their hands enthusiastically in the warm air, as their eyes squinted into the sunset.

"Well, I'm pretty impressed with this little girl," I continued. I pointed out that she knew what it was like to have something dreadfully unfair happen in life. She had been grabbed from her home and all that was familiar to her. Were any of her brothers or sisters taken at the same time? What about her parents? Did she have to watch them be killed as her dad fought to save them all? We don't know.

Then came the days, if not weeks, of walking. Every step took her farther from home. She probably had to sleep on the ground. She was no doubt upset and exhausted, crying quietly over the loss of her freedom and her family. What would become of her in this strange land?

She wound up being forced into slavery at Naaman's house. Day after day, she had to work, perhaps from dawn to dark. She had no control over her life anymore.

She learned that her master was a big shot in the Aramean military; it was his troops who had raided her town and swept her away. But she also found out that her master had a physical problem, a chronic skin disease for which there was no cure.

Did she say to herself, *Serves him right for his cruelty to me and my people?* Did she say to herself, *I hope he dies an agonizing death over this?*

No, with a heart of childlike goodwill, she commented to Naaman's wife, "I wish my master would go to see the prophet in Samaria. He would heal him of his leprosy" (2 Kings 5:3).

What's going on here? It is natural to want payback when something bad happens to you. And you can always find someone to sympathize with you. But this little girl shows us a different approach. She chose to forgive rather than seek revenge. Then she even offered her help.

We don't have to like the hurtful actions of others. In fact, we should put a stop to them if we can. But if that proves impractical, we can still forgive. God may even use us to bring about great change in the offender's life.

As you probably know, Naaman and his wife listened to the hostage girl's advice. He ended up making a trip to see the prophet she had mentioned. In the end (after some initial confusion), the general was miraculously healed. He returned to Aram with gratitude and a softened spirit.

We don't know if he rewarded the little girl for her kindness. It would be nice to read that he set her free and returned her to her village in Israel. The Bible doesn't say that. It says only that good things happened because a victim declined to seek revenge.

I went on to tell the Wichita crowd about our experience with "57," the captor with the bad attitude whom I mentioned in my first book. About twenty-three years old, he was average height for a Filipino—maybe five foot six, and not especially muscular. Yet he had been tapped to carry a heavy rocket launcher called an M57— thus, his nickname.

The young man was always sullen, complaining, and argumentative. His English was not strong, so I wasn't able to learn much about him, why he had joined the Abu Sayyaf, or what his personal dreams were. All I knew, as I told Martin once, was that the nickname fit because the kid had been in a bad mood for fifty-seven days straight! Martin chuckled.

With a little detective work though, Martin eventually found out that "57" suffered from serious headaches. His surliness was not so much caused by the load he carried as by his pounding head. Martin began to offer him pain relievers from our little stash.

The fellow's attitude toward Martin changed instantly. From that moment on, my husband was his friend.

Not long afterward, the Abu Sayyaf sent "57" out on a raiding expedition, and he was gone for several weeks. When he returned, he promptly gave Martin the full greeting used in this part of the world, a kiss on each cheek. A big smile lit up his face.

We eventually lost track of "57" at a rubber plantation when word came that the government's marines were on our trail. This young captor was chosen to go scouting and find out if this was true. The Abu Sayyaf gave him a nice haircut so he would look like a "city boy" on his expedition. We never saw him again. But to this day, I have a warm spot in my heart for that young man because of what Martin did for him.

Jesus said, "If you are willing to listen, I say, love your enemies. Do good to those who hate you. . . . If someone slaps you on one cheek, turn the other cheek. If someone demands your coat, offer your shirt also" (Luke 6:27, 29).

Jesus wasn't just speaking hyperbole. He really meant it. And he put it into practice himself, on the night of his arrest in the garden of Gethsemane. He was about to lose all control over his life and be taken into custody. I love the way Phillip Keller describes this moment in his book *Rabboni:*

> At this point Peter whipped out his sword. He never was a coward. The big strong-muscled fisherman was quick to take advantage of the situation. The sharp steel flashed in the flickering light of the flares. There was an anguished scream. Malchus, a servant of the high priest, held his hand to his head. Hot blood gushed from the severed stump of his ear. An inch or two farther over and his skull would have been split in half by Peter's angry stroke.
>
> Jesus was quick to take it all in.
>
> "Put away your sword, Peter!" His command was short and sharp. "He who lives by violence dies by violence." This was not the place or time for a show of strength. . . .
>
> The Master, meanwhile, reached out quietly and touched Malchus. The wound was healed: the ear restored: the blood stanched.

Here is the paragraph that really gets my attention.

> It was the last miracle of healing Jesus was to
> perform. And He did it to the man who came out
> to help lynch Him in the dark.[3]

You and I have a choice. We can do things our way or God's way. In the case of Naaman, God received glory because a little girl did the right thing. In the garden, a personal tragedy was reversed because the Son of God did the right thing.

Revenge has a way of making ugly situations uglier. The stakes are raised, the emotions are heightened, and before you know it, the pain has been multiplied in all directions. How many people have filed a lawsuit or taken some other vindictive step, only to look back five years later and wistfully say, "I wish I hadn't done that. It just made matters worse."

How much better to do something truly radical . . . to step outside the pattern of tit-for-tat, to return good for evil, and to watch the surprise on people's faces. It frees them up to think in new and healthier ways. It keeps our own spirit clean. And it honors our heavenly Father, who taught us to love the most unlovely of all.

6

*Worry
Doesn't
Help*

Since coming home I've met dozens of people who have said to me, "I was so worried about you and Martin all that time." With good intentions, they want me to know that their thoughts were with us during the year of captivity.

They assume, additionally, that I was worried, too. It would be only human nature in such a predicament.

Well, yes, I admit that I worried—although not about some of the things you might suppose.

I decided early on that I wouldn't worry about the kids. I knew that our mission's policy was to evacuate family members out of harm's way as soon as possible. So within a few days of capture, I told myself that Jeff, Mindy, and Zach were no doubt back in the United States. That turned out to be true; they spent the year with Grandpa and Grandma Burnham.

Meanwhile in the steamy jungle, I didn't have the energy to worry about them, so I made a conscious decision not to do so. I would wonder about them, of course. I'd hike along the trail calculating in my mind what time it was back in Kansas and try to imagine what they might be doing. Morning in the Philippines was the previous evening in America; had the kids gone to bed yet? Were they lying there thinking about us or about something else? What would they get to do for fun that Friday night? When would they see my parents next?

As time went on, we began to get a few letters from them. These were the highlight of our life. Martin and I read them aloud to each other more than once. They filled in a lot of the blanks in our minds.

A different topic for worry, especially for Martin, was the New Tribes Mission flight program across the Philippines. He had been the chief pilot, responsible for everything from personnel to safety training to government paperwork. All of the pilots looked to him for direction.

He had almost finished writing a new training manual, more than a hundred pages long. We were at the proofreading stage, in fact. And now he was totally cut off. Nobody could ask him any questions. All the wealth of data in his brain was out of reach.

Eventually we came to the reluctant conclusion that there was not a single thing we could do about the flight program now. Others would have to step up to the responsibility, so why worry about it?

Instead, we found other, more immediate things to make us anxious.

Every time I picked out the words "low batt!" amid the various dialects of Abu Sayyaf chatter, my stomach began to churn. Low battery in the cell phone or the satellite phone meant that our only link to the outside world was about to fade. If the captors could not talk to their comrades in town, we might run out of food. If the captors could not talk to the government officials, negotiation would stall.

Even though Martin had tutored them on how to recharge their phones using a string of C-size batteries, they didn't always remember to do so. The flickering current of those little cylinders was our lifeline. It always irritated me to hear the young guys asking for batteries to run their radios, just so they could listen to music, instead of saving the power for phone use.

I have already written about how traumatized I was whenever the AFP (Armed Forces of the Philippines) began lobbing artillery shells at our camp. The whistle of incoming fire was eerie; we knew we could explode in a blazing inferno any second. Death rode atop those shells.

And the whole tactic was so wrongheaded! This was clearly no way to pluck vulnerable hostages out of a dangerous environment. The AFP was unleashing a no-holds-barred assault that would incinerate terrorists and victims alike if their aim was good enough. The army didn't seem to be thinking clearly. They were just blasting away with their weaponry, not calculating the possible harm to us.

Yes, I worried. But in the end, no artillery shell ever landed close enough to affect us. God in his mercy spared us from that kind of fiery demolition.

E. Stanley Jones, the Methodist missionary to India, wrote a devotional entitled "Worry Is Atheism" just as World War II was heating up. He was away from his wife and family on a trip, and a well-meaning hostess said to him one evening, "You have had a quiet day; you've had time to worry." Jones writes:

> I felt inwardly startled. "Time to worry"—as if a Christian ever has "time to worry"! The Christian has expunged worry from his vocabulary. . . .
>
> A person who worries says, "I cannot trust God; I'll take things into my own hands." Result? Worry, frustration, incapacity to meet the dreaded thing when it does come. With God, you can meet it, overcome it, assimilate it into the purpose of your life. Alone, you fuss and fume and are frustrated.
>
> Worry says, "God doesn't care, and so He won't do anything—I'll have to worry it through." Faith says, "God does care, and He and I will work it out together. I'll supply the willingness, and He will supply the power—with that combination we can do anything."

And then Jones tells a wonderful story about the great reformer Martin Luther:

> One morning, when he was blue and discouraged, his wife appeared [clothed] in black. At Luther's inquiry as to what the mourning meant, she replied, "Haven't you heard? God is dead."
>
> Luther saw the absurdity—and so should you. God lives—so will you![4]

One dictionary definition of *worry* is "to torment oneself with disturbing thoughts."[5] The active verb form

is interesting, isn't it? Worry is something *we do to
ourselves*. It is not an involuntary twitch, an allergic
reaction to some mysterious chemical, a spell that is cast
upon us from the outside. We initiate the worrying. We
torment ourselves.

What we start, we can also stop.

The word's roots trace back to the Old English
wyrgan, "to strangle." That is precisely what worry does
to us; it cuts off our air. It prevents us from inhaling the
Divine Breath, the Holy Spirit of God. Instead, it slowly
asphyxiates us.

Have you ever sensed that your life was steadily shriv-
eling, closing in upon itself because of a worry spasm?
You could no longer see the sun, the hope, the joy of
life. Your entire field of vision was consumed with the
problem.

In my dictionary, the word *worry* comes just after
wormwood and *worn-out*. Right behind it comes *worse*
and *worst*. What an awful page!

What an awful waste of mental energy.

The antidote to worry, as everyone who has ever read
the familiar Philippians 4:6-7 knows, is to turn to the
Lord. "Don't worry about anything; instead, pray about
everything. Tell God what you need, and thank him for
all he has done. If you do this, you will experience God's
peace. . . ."

It sounds commonplace, I know. But it is still true.

A unique, perhaps quaint, phrase keeps showing up

over a stretch of six chapters in 1 Chronicles: to "inquire of the LORD." This phrase seems to make all the difference in the outcome of King Saul versus King David. Of the first, this sad epitaph is recorded: "Saul died because he was unfaithful to the LORD; he did not keep the word of the LORD and even consulted a medium for guidance, and *did not inquire of the LORD*. So the LORD put him to death and turned the kingdom over to David son of Jesse" (10:13-14).

One of David's first moves upon ascending the throne was to rescue the Ark of the Covenant from the fringes of national life. "'Let us bring the ark of our God back to us, for *we did not inquire of it* during the reign of Saul.' The whole assembly agreed to do this, because it seemed right to all the people" (13:3-4).

When the pagan Philistines came up to raid Israel, "David *inquired of God* . . . [and] the LORD answered him" (14:10). The Israelites won the battle.

But the Philistines soon came back. "So David *inquired of God again,* and God answered him" (14:14) with an odd set of military instructions about waiting for a certain sound in the treetops before launching the attack. It worked.

The first attempt to bring the Ark to Jerusalem had faltered on a violation of procedure, and at the second attempt David explained, "It was because you, the Levites, did not bring it up the first time that the LORD our God broke out in anger against us. *We did not inquire of him* about how to do it in the prescribed way" (15:13). This time, the effort was a huge success. In the psalm

David wrote for the gala occasion, he included these lyrics: *"Look to the LORD and his strength; seek his face always"* (16:11; all 1 Chronicles citations from the New International Version; italics added).

This was the modus operandi of the greatest monarch Israel ever knew. Repeatedly, consistently, even incessantly, he "inquired of the Lord." The response to that inquiry brought calmness, clarity, and wisdom.

God does not mean for us to sit and fret, stew, agonize, wring our hands, or be troubled. Instead, he invites us to interact with him, to gain his perspective, and to rest in his good and perfect will for our lives.

In the jungle I quickly realized that in order to keep pace with the others on the trail, I was going to need a considerable supply of drinking water. When I didn't have it, my face would begin to flush, my mouth would go dry, and fatigue would set in rapidly. I would plead with Solaiman or Hurayra or another captor, "Please, I need water. Can you get me some water?"

I would also beg God. "Lord, I need water. It's really bad. God, help me! I need water." I was imploring him over and over, almost frantically. I was hammering on heaven's door.

My anxiety would rise another notch when I watched the Abu Sayyaf using up precious water for purely ceremonial purposes, such as washing their feet or their face before evening prayers. Not being Muslim, I found this to be wholly unnecessary. What a waste of the resource I craved so badly.

Then one day on the trail, as I was harassing God

once again, it began to dawn upon me that he knew very well about my need for hydration. He wasn't oblivious to that fact. My prayers gradually changed from, "God, *water—now!*" to "Lord, you know what I need. You understand my body's need for water. Help me be patient until you take care of my need."

And he did. Not long after, a captor named Zacarias gave me my very own water bottle! It was made of translucent plastic, with a handle and a red top; it held about a liter. I could fill it up myself every time we came to a stream, and no one would take it away from me or ask to use it. I felt God had restored my ability to control the situation.

God is big enough to make his own decisions and manage his own actions. He doesn't have to run everything by us before he acts. He is in charge, and we are not. If he doesn't need to worry about the current state of affairs (and obviously he doesn't), then neither do we.

7

Rising
above Impatience

My secretary's husband is a pharmacist. All day long he has the job of carefully measuring and packaging medicines for people. Prescriptions arrive on slips of paper (in doctors' notorious scrawl) or by telephone, and people want their pills as quickly as possible. Yet he knows that hurry can cause mistakes, which in his line of work could be deadly.

This pharmacist has been in the business long enough to notice a pattern.

"The terminally ill are the most patient," he says. "If I'm out of a certain medicine, they don't get upset. They know I'll get more as soon as I can. If there's some kind of glitch in our computer system so that they have to wait an extra ten minutes for their medicine, that's all right. They stay kind.

"In contrast, somebody with a runny nose can be standing there tapping their fingers on the counter like, *C'mon, c'mon, whatsa matter with you, anyway? I need my stuff, now!*"

I was intrigued with his analysis. It reminded me that the difficulties of life have a way of clarifying what is truly important. In the jungle, I found that my walk with

God and my relationship with my family were the big items. Waiting a few extra minutes was certainly not.

That is what the epistle of James is saying when it opens with these words: "The trying of your faith worketh patience. But let patience have her perfect work, that ye may be perfect and entire, wanting nothing" (James 1:3-4, KJV). When life spins out of control and we can no longer manage our circumstances, we are forced to become more long-suffering, less demanding, more serene. It is an unfortunate way to have to learn this lesson, but it works.

Impatience is a way of saying, *I'm important. My needs and my schedule ought to take priority here. Whatever is happening in another person's life doesn't rank quite as high as mine.*

We make such a sweeping conclusion without actually knowing the rest of the facts. We haven't learned what is causing the delay; we just know we don't like it and we're going to exercise our all-American right to crab about it.

I used to be a fairly impatient person. I just called it by other names—say, "efficient" or "productive." If I walked into McDonald's at 10:03 A.M., and they hadn't yet switched over from the breakfast menu to the lunch menu, I would ask for the manager. "Sir, your sign says you change menus at 10 o'clock. So why can't I get a hamburger and fries? What's the problem here?"

I'm so ashamed when I think back to those days. I was

always pushing people, expecting perfection from everyone.

And then came the jungle year, when food was more hit-and-miss than I had ever imagined. I couldn't get a hamburger at 10 in the morning, at noon, at 6 in the evening, or any other time. I had to learn a whole new dimension of patience.

People have laughed at my story in the first book about the time I asked God for a hamburger, thinking that would only be possible if he turned us free in the city. Finally, I got my hamburger from Jollibee (the Philippine fast-food chain) one night near Zamboanga—but I still didn't have my freedom. That is when I realized that God could do anything, even outlandish things. But he wasn't going to be pressured.

My prayer thereafter began to change. "Lord, whatever you have to teach us in this situation, let us learn it," I prayed. "You know how badly I want to get out of this predicament. But even more than that, I want what you want. I want the character of spiritual maturity. I want the fruits of the Holy Spirit—one of which is patience (see Galatians 5:22). Work in my heart and life, O Lord."

During college, my roommate Margie introduced me to the Henry Drummond classic entitled *The Greatest Thing in the World*. It is a marvelous exposition of 1 Corinthians 13 by a Scotsman who worked with D. L. Moody in the late 1800s. I used to reread that book once a year, until eventually I lost my copy.

After a theoretical treatment of the components of love, Drummond writes:

> So much for the analysis of love. Now the business of our lives is to have these things fitted into our characters. That is the supreme work to which we need to address ourselves in this world. Is life not full of opportunities for learning love? Every man and woman every day has a thousand of them. The world is not a playground, it is a schoolroom. Life is not a holiday, but an education. The one eternal lesson for us all is *how better we can love*.
>
> What makes a person a good cricketer? Practice. What makes a person a good artist, a good sculptor, a good musician? Practice. What makes a person a good linguist, a good stenographer? Practice. What makes a person a good person? Practice. Nothing else. . . .
>
> What was Christ doing in the carpenter's shop? Practicing. Though perfect, we read that *He* learned obedience, and grew in wisdom and in favor with God. Do not quarrel, therefore, with your lot in life. Do not complain of its never-ceasing cares, its petty environment, the vexations you have to stand, the small and sordid souls you have to live with and work with. Above all, do not resent temptation, and do not be perplexed because it seems to thicken round you more and more, and ceases neither through effort, agony, or prayer. That is your practice. That is the practice that God

appoints you—and it is having its work in making you patient, humble, generous, unselfish, kind, and courteous.[6]

By now, you can tell that I am frequently affected by music. Here is another case: We were in church on a Sunday morning singing, "Nearer, My God, to Thee." The opening stanza says something startling: "Nearer, my God, to Thee; nearer to Thee! / E'en though it be a cross that raiseth me."

The writer, Sarah F. Adams, was proclaiming that she wanted to be lifted up as close to God in heaven as she could get, even if the means of elevation—the hoist, if you will—had to be a cross! If crucifixion was what it took to be nearer to her God, so be it.

I don't know that I could honestly say that. I don't like to suffer. I never choose discomfort over comfort.

During our year of captivity, FBI agents interviewed our kids in Kansas. "We can't imagine how Mom is surviving all this time," they told the men. "She doesn't even like to camp!"

Would I choose to deny myself and camp for a year to get closer to God? That's hardly my style.

But it does bring to mind what Paul wrote in Galatians: "I have been crucified with Christ. I myself no longer live, but Christ lives in me. So I live my life in this earthly body by trusting in the Son of God, who loved me and gave himself for me. I am not one of those who treats the grace of God as meaningless" (2:19-21).

This must have been a shocking thought to Paul's original readers in the Roman Empire, many of whom had watched actual crucifixions. Yes, it had happened to Jesus—a horrific atrocity. But here the apostle was venturing into something else entirely. He said he felt crucified, at least in some metaphorical way. His will, his person, his selfishness had been executed in order that new, divine life and character might replace them.

A page or two later in his epistle, immediately after the fruit-of-the-Spirit listing mentioned earlier, Paul added: "Those who belong to Christ Jesus have nailed the passions and desires of their sinful nature to his cross and crucified them there. If we are living now by the Holy Spirit, let us follow the Holy Spirit's leading in every part of our lives" (5:24-25).

Every part of our lives? Even our schedule? Even our yearning for action, for progress, for achievement, for resolution to our difficulty? Yes. The call to patience is a divine call, a summons to get in rhythm with God's pace instead of the human way. It is a hard adjustment to make, but it yields many benefits.

8

Weakness Is Normal

Not long ago I saw an ad for an exercise class in our little town—"lower-body strength," it promised. I had never done any physical therapy for the leg that had been shot when I was rescued, so I thought this class might be a good idea. I signed up.

Every Thursday morning after I drop the kids at school, I join seven or eight other women in the basement of the old Methodist church building. We groan and strain for an hour as our instructor, Susie, pushes us to our limit. We also do a fair share of talking and laughing. But, in fact, I think my leg is getting stronger these days.

No one—young or old, male or female—aspires to be "weak." Whether we are physically fit or haven't seen the inside of a workout gym in decades, we inherently pass an electronic scanner over the terrain of our personalities looking for readings of "strong." Can't bench-press 350 pounds? No, but I'm really good at holding my tongue under pressure. Can't run a mile without stopping for extra breath? No, but I can get three kids fed and out the door to school on time without a hitch.

We like the word *strong*. We embrace it in a thousand

different ways. We take it as a compliment. It means we're on top of things, in charge, competent, capable.

Like a football player who sprained his ankle in practice last week but doesn't want the other team to know, we do our best to conceal our weaknesses. We posture as if everything is fine. We look composed and ready. We silently steel ourselves to give no hint of the flaw that lies within. What "they" don't know ("they" being the boss, the coworker, the friend, or even a family member), they don't need to know.

There is One who knows all, of course. He is entirely aware of our physical, mental, moral, and spiritual fitness. "He understands how weak we are; he knows we are only dust," says Psalm 103:14. That is why the previous verse says, "The LORD is like a father to his children, tender and compassionate to those who fear him."

He is not fooled by our pretensions of adequacy. He knows full well that in the human condition, weakness is universal. It is normal. It is par for the course.

And that is why, in order to connect with us, he sent his Son as a common human being. "He made himself nothing; he took the humble position of a slave and appeared in human form" (Philippians 2:7). Thus Jesus knows everything about our frailty. He experienced the queasiness of facing a challenge that appeared too big to handle. He felt our anxieties and fears.

Last Christmastime, I was driving somewhere with the radio on, and the familiar carol "Thou Didst Leave Thy Throne" began to play. I've always loved that song. Suddenly in the third stanza, a line jumped out at me:

The foxes found rest, and the birds their nest
In the shade of the forest tree;
But thy couch was the sod, O Thou Son of God,
In the deserts of Galilee.[7]   (emphasis mine)

It's talking about Jesus sleeping on the hard ground at night. I could instantly identify. Martin and I spent three and a half months sleeping on the jungle floor, until Janjalani, the Abu Sayyaf's leader, left the camp one day and gave us his hammock. Until then, it was hard to get comfortable at night. How was it that my ribs inevitably found the protruding roots? No matter how much we prepared the site, moving twigs and stones out of the way, things seemed to "grow" during the night. I squirmed and scooted until it felt better, but an hour later, the bumps were poking me again.

When morning finally came, I didn't feel rested. I started the new day in a condition of weakness. I was not at my full power. And I knew that the next night was not going to be any more refreshing or rejuvenating than the last one.

My only choice was to lean upon the Lord for an extra measure of his strength.

Growing up as the fifth child in a family of six, I learned early to take care of myself, not to ask for help unless it was absolutely necessary, and always to present myself as strong. This stance, of course, is not a bad thing. Self-sufficiency is a value worth pursuing.

When Martin and I went to the mission field without the many props of modern American life, it was essential to take charge of our needs, to make do, to find ways of solving our own problems. At one point our town was under a severe water shortage. For several hours a day, the faucets produced only a trickle. We made trips to the spring a half mile away to get drinking water. We saved wash water to flush toilets.

Another time, the whole town was out of margarine. None could be bought anywhere. We learned that if you spread a bit of oil on your toast and then sprinkled salt on top, it didn't taste too bad. Creativity was our motto.

Only rarely did I let down. One time was just a couple of months after Jeffrey was born, when I contracted malaria. No matter how much I wanted to take care of my new baby, I could not. I could only lie in bed in a state of utter helplessness. Some of the time, I was hallucinating from the high fever. I was of no good to anyone.

For three days or so, another missionary wife came and took Jeffrey to her home for care. She would bring my precious child to my side every three hours for nursing, and that was all. Even so, my temperature was so high that by the end of feeding him, his little body would be drenched in sweat from my heat. I felt like such an inadequate mother.

But soon I recovered and got back on top of things. I resumed my standard pattern of being "strong" . . . until the day we were captured by the Abu Sayyaf. And then, within a day or two, I figured out that I was the weakest person, at least physically, in this whole ragged brigade.

The young warriors could seemingly hike forever with no food. Even the other Filipino hostages could actually enjoy a bath in a cold mountain stream. My husband could tie a perfect knot. And then at the bottom of the totem pole was pathetic little Gracia, who couldn't do any of those things.

I learned that God is the same tower of strength whether you are going through a valley or reaching the mountaintop. The familiar psalm says, "Yea, though I walk the valley of the shadow of death, I will fear no evil: for thou art with me; thy rod and thy staff they comfort me" (23:4, KJV). God has the ability to snatch you out of the evil of the valley. Sometimes, however, he simply goes with you *through* the valley.

As the saying goes, "Sometimes God calms the storm, but sometimes he calms you." He has the power to prevent storms altogether, of course. But in his infinite wisdom, he sometimes allows storms to rage so that he can achieve a greater end. He explained it to a distressed apostle this way: "My gracious favor is all you need. My power works best in your weakness." Paul then con-cluded, "So now I am glad to boast about my weaknesses, so that the power of Christ may work through me. Since I know it is all for Christ's good, I am quite content with my weaknesses and with insults, hardships, persecutions, and calamities. For when I am weak, then I am strong" (2 Corinthians 12:9-10).

Jim Cymbala's first months as a young and ill-prepared pastor at the Brooklyn Tabernacle were awful. Nothing was going right in this woeful congregation of twenty or so people in a rundown, inner-city building. Bills were stacking up, dissension rumbled through the little group, and growth was nil.

One Sunday night, Cymbala was no more than five minutes into his sermon when the shabbiness of it all overwhelmed him to the point that he could not continue. "I'm sorry—I just can't go on preaching," he confessed to the people. Tears rose up in his eyes. He closed his Bible and with embarrassment asked the congregation to come join him for prayer at the front of the church.

They shuffled forward, and all was quiet for a time. Then slowly, genuine calls to heaven began to arise. Both pastor and parishioners pled with God to take over and make their church what it could be. Cymbala writes:

> When I was at my lowest, confounded by obstacles . . . I discovered an astonishing truth: God is attracted to weakness. He can't resist those who humbly and honestly admit how desperately they need him. Our weakness, in fact, makes room for his power.[8]

I have those words taped to the full-length mirror in my bedroom so I can read them every day of my life. Without the Lord, I can do nothing. He waits for me to admit my shortcomings so that he can then invade with his supernatural power.

Today, the Brooklyn Tabernacle is a beacon of light in New York City, with some 12,000 attending each

Sunday. The music of the church's choir, led by Jim's wife, is world famous. Jim and Carol Cymbala still say, after thirty years, that prayer and reliance upon God are the secret of everything they do. The church's Tuesday night prayer meeting draws thousands in earnest appeal to the God of heaven to reach down and affect desperate situations.

God is the faithful One when we're not. He is the changeless One who knows the end from the beginning. He knows us, including our weaknesses, better than anyone else, because he created us. When our fragile world breaks up in a dozen pieces, he is not surprised. He stands ever ready to see us through.

9

We All Fall Down

It was a strange family outing, I admit, but fortunately my kids didn't balk. "I want us all to go visit Haven of Hope," I announced one evening. "It's a shelter for the homeless in Wichita, and I think it would be good for us to get in touch with that kind of ministry."

They said, "Okay, Mom. Sounds good to us, as long as it doesn't take all day." So on the appointed Saturday we piled into the van and headed to the edge of the city. There in what looked like a former nursing home, the Union Rescue Mission had set up this center. They ran buses from downtown Wichita late each afternoon, bringing in men who had no other place to eat or sleep.

The first order of business for the arriving men, we learned, was a shower. Then came a gospel service in the large meeting area, followed by a meal. Finally, everyone dispersed down the long hallways to sleep in the many rooms of the building. They would be bused back downtown the next morning, since some of them had day-labor jobs.

I had gotten the idea for an excursion like this one day in the jungle, when I said to Martin, "You know, I don't ever want to forget what it's like to be hungry.

This feeling—it's real for too many millions of people in the world. When we get out of here, I want to take the kids to a rescue mission somewhere."

I didn't have any place in mind. Then a few months after my return to America, we were at the Kansas State Fair in Hutchinson, and I spied a booth for Haven of Hope. I walked up, introduced myself to some of the women working there, and asked if I could bring my family for a tour. They said yes.

After the visit, we were impressed enough with their program that we talked about it back in our church in Rose Hill. In time, our pastor invited the Union Rescue Mission to send a guest speaker to our Sunday evening service. He stayed for the youth group that meets afterward in the basement. This meeting always starts with food—sloppy joes with chips and pop that evening, as I recall—and then the man spoke about keeping your life clean from drugs and alcohol so as not to end up being one of his clients.

I'll never forget what happened in the question-and-answer time afterward. Various kids made comments, including my Jeff and Mindy. From the fringe where I sat, I could see one girl fidgeting, as if she wanted to say something but wasn't sure she should.

Then the leader called on her. "Tell us what you're thinking," he said.

She brushed her hair back and said, "You don't want to know."

"Yes, we do," came the reply. "What's on your mind?"

"Well," she answered with a bit of detachment, "the

way I look at it, these people you talk about have made bad choices. And now they're reaping the consequences. I'm not sure it's our duty to get them out of their own trouble."

The room was quiet for a moment. The speaker didn't react or launch into any defense of his organization. What happened next was that I spoke up, even though I was a mom, not one of the teenagers. "You know, it's when we're in trouble—whether or not it's our fault—that we need grace," I said quietly.

"Without realizing it, I made a bad choice when I arranged for my husband and me to go to Dos Palmas that Saturday. If I hadn't chosen that resort, we would never have been kidnapped. I would still have Martin to live with. All kinds of things would be different today if I hadn't started down a treacherous road.

"But when we found ourselves in a mess, we needed help, and we needed it badly. The way I look at it, sooner or later we're all going to need the grace of God in our life, to compensate for our mistakes."

The discussion continued along this line for a while, and I kept thinking about the fact that our choice to sin is much worse than any selection of a getaway resort. Sin separates us from God, and that is the worst predicament of all.

When we were needy, we needed a ransom. Second Corinthians 8:9 says, "You know how full of love and kindness our Lord Jesus Christ was. Though he was very rich, yet for your sakes he became poor, so that by his poverty he could make you rich." Jesus left his heavenly palaces, where he was praised night and day, to come to this nasty earth and pay our ransom. He lived among us and let himself be killed by human hands so we could be redeemed.

The Mother Goose rhyme "Ring Around the Rosie" ends with this line: "We all fall down." In real life, we dance and prance our way along, but sooner or later, all of us seem to go splat on the ground for one reason or another. Then what?

Our only hope is for God's grace. He sees us lying there, scuffed and bruised. He is entirely willing to help us up, dust us off, and stabilize us again. In fact, attitude makes a lot of difference. "The LORD mocks at mockers," says Proverbs 3:34, "but he shows favor to the humble." This verse is referenced *twice* in the New Testament, once in James 4:6, then again in 1 Peter 5:5. Apparently, it is a key theme of Scripture.

The humbling experiences of life are meant to introduce us to God's favor. Surely God's people can do no less than to exemplify this favor to others in real, tangible ways. And when we ourselves need to receive this grace, the best thing we can do is simply relax our taut shoulders and open our hands.

If we expect to get all the way through life without embarrassing ourselves, without playing the fool, without needing the unmerited favor of God . . . well, it's just not going to happen. We are too human—all of us.

I remember one sultry morning in the jungle when

Martin and I were packing up for a day on the move. It was sometime after Thanksgiving, because we had a now-empty plastic Skippy peanut-butter jar from our recent care package that we were using to carry whatever morsels of food our captors would give us. It was often *viand,* the Filipino term for anything that goes with rice. It could be chopped bananas boiled in coconut milk with salt or onions or garlic, for example. Or it could be boiled squash. Sometimes on a farm we'd find ginger roots that we could chop up for added flavor.

On this day, we had received our portion, and I remember twisting the lid onto the jar. As I picked it up to place it in my backpack, the lid came off. Apparently I hadn't gotten it on straight. The jar fell to the ground, dumping out all the *viand.* That was to have been our food for the whole day!

A sick feeling swept over me. I looked up at Martin and said, "Oh, I am so, so sorry! I've just dropped our food." I started to cry.

He looked at the wet spot on the ground, then turned to me and said, "I forgive you . . . and you need to forgive yourself."

I learned a lot about grace and forgiveness that day. I learned that my husband was more prepared to absolve me of my clumsiness than I was. In fact, he would have to pay the same price I was going to pay. We would both go hungry that day as we trudged along the trail. Yet there was not a flicker of blame in his eyes.

That is how it is when we come to our heavenly Father in the wake of a wrong move. He extends his love and restoration to our souls. And he wants us to do the same for ourselves.

I have noticed that as we give grace to ourselves and to one another, it becomes a way of life. Maybe that is why my son Jeff kept his cool when I did just about the worst thing a teenager's mother can do to him: I backed out of the garage without looking in the rearview mirror and crunched right into his pride and joy, his little blue Dodge Neon in the driveway.

Jeff was in the van with me, and we got out to survey the damage. Once again, I felt so stupid. The bumper of the van had put a big crease down the left side of his car. His side mirror was hanging by a cord. He couldn't get the left door open.

In that awful moment, my sixteen-year-old son, like his father, gave me grace. There was a soft sigh, and then he said, "It's okay, Mom. We'll get it fixed."

I could have hugged him. But the neighbors were no doubt watching.

I apologized every way I knew and said, yes, we'd certainly get it repaired. When I called the insurance agent to file the claim, however, things got complicated. Jeff and I had titled the car in both our names since he was not yet of adult age. "I'm sorry, Mrs. Burnham," said the lady on the other end, "but you can't claim damage against your own property if you caused it."

"But it's Jeff's car!" I cried.

"Yes, I know. But on the official record of the state,

it's your car, too. If a tree had fallen on it or something, that would be a different story. Self-inflicted damage, on the other hand, doesn't qualify for coverage."

I had no choice but to pay the body shop out of my own pocket. We were heading into Christmastime, with all its expenses, and here the repair was going to run more than a thousand dollars. I gulped and signed the work order.

At that point, I faced a choice. I could go home and beat myself up for wasting a big chunk of money, getting a migraine in the process. Or I could forgive myself and believe that something good would come of it all somehow.

I still don't know what that good might be (other than providing an expensive illustration for this chapter!). I do know, however, that it served to remind me once again that we all need grace.

In a way, I guess I'm a little like Peter in the Bible. Like me, he talked a lot. He was proud and thought he knew so much. Frequently, he said the wrong thing. If he had come with me to one of Mindy's basketball games, I can just imagine the two of us sitting there on the bleachers yelling at the refs.

On the night of Jesus' arrest, Peter denied even knowing the Lord three times. Imagine what this man had to face when he looked in a mirror.

We know the Lord Jesus forgave him; the story by the seaside in John 21, when Jesus asked Peter three times if he loved him, is one of the Bible's most touching. And apparently Peter forgave himself, becoming a respected apostle. Decades later, his written instruction to other leaders in 1 Peter 5 is mature and valuable. After quoting the Old Testament proverb mentioned earlier, he adds, "So humble yourselves under the mighty power of God, and in his good time he will honor you" (verse 6).

We all mess up. We all fall down. We all self-destruct at times. And we all need to open up and receive the warm, restoring grace that originates with our loving Lord.

10

No Losers

One type of disaster is worse than all others—perhaps not always in its consequences, but in the internal pain it wreaks. That is the disaster we make ourselves.

It is one thing to be minding our own business in life, only to get slammed with an illness or a job loss or some other reversal. It is quite another to torpedo ourselves through an undeniable mistake. The person who steps outside of his or her marriage . . . the trusted employee who mishandles corporate funds . . . the boyfriend and girlfriend who unthinkingly conceive a child one Saturday night . . . the young man who rejects his faith and turns instead to drugs or alcohol . . . the person who betrays a longtime friend. These are not cases of "It happened to me." These are cases of "I did it."

The fallout may be swift, or not. If it is slow, we may rationalize our actions for a while. We don't like to admit that we messed up. We stall as long as we can. Only when outside realities force us to the ugly truth do we admit it. Only when a spouse explodes in enlightened rage, or the police move in, or the doctor confirms that a baby is indeed on the way, do we grudgingly confess what has been going on.

What is sometimes hard for us to appreciate at this point is that more than just fate is working against us. It is more than a matter of our luck running out. Behind the scenes, God is at work, quietly but irresistibly bringing us to his mirror to get a close-up look at what we're really like. The events of our life are his pressure bars, gradually nudging us where we would not otherwise go, until we are confronted with ourselves.

Then what happens? Once we own up to the fact that we have thrown our own life into a tailspin, is everything lost? Is there any hope to regain our balance? What does God think of his errant child?

While we were living and working in Malaybalay during the 1990s, an ugly thing was exposed at one of our mission schools. It didn't affect our three children; I was homeschooling them at the time. But it touched the lives of many other families. We were all saddened and upset as the individual was sent back to the States, dismissed from further service.

I remember going to church one Sunday morning with a heavy heart. Our church was on the main street near the top of a hill, and the whine of the *jeepneys* (minibuses) and the *motorelas* (motorcycle taxis with a sidecar) chugging up the slope came through the open windows. I slipped into my seat hoping to find some calm.

The service began. I was still rumbling inside with frustration. I found it hard to concentrate during worship.

And then a good friend of mine, Joy Santa Maria,

stood up to sing a solo, a new song at the time entitled "In Heaven's Eyes." The words by Phill McHugh grabbed my attention. They described a hurting person's cry to God. The longer Joy sang, the more I was moved by the Lord's response to this anonymous individual: "Gazing down on this unlovely one, there was love in heaven's eyes."

I sat there thinking deeply about the "unlovely one" whose deeds had so exasperated us all. The song was forcing me to try to view him through heaven's eyes instead of my own. I didn't want to do that, but I knew I should.

By the time I had listened to the chorus the second time ("In heaven's eyes, there are no losers"[9]), tears were streaming down my face. I could not escape the fact that God's grace is available to help us all in our time of need. The offender, if he will ask for it . . . the victim, if he wants it. God does not look down from heaven and pick only some to receive his grace. He freely extends it to all. Jesus taught us in the Sermon on the Mount, "Your Father in heaven . . . gives his sunlight to both the evil and the good, and he sends rain on the just and on the unjust, too" (Matthew 5:45).

I could not get away from the fact that even if we have created our own chaos, God knows and listens. He sees the fiasco, and he feels the pain of disappointment. His response is not anger but rather compassion.

I knew in my heart that I had to forgive this person. It was very hard. If I stiffened my back against forgiveness, not only would I be disobedient but the smoldering anger would sap my strength. I had to let go of righteous indignation and recognize that God's grace was big enough to forgive and heal.

In other words, I had to remain humble and aware of my own tendency to sin. Even though what had happened was not my sin, it would *engender* sin if I hardened my heart against the individual. I prayed, "Lord, how can I forgive this sinner?" And the answer came loud and clear: "Forgive us our sins, just as we have forgiven those who have sinned against us" (Matthew 6:12).

I chose in that moment to forgive. I don't think I drummed up the forgiveness from within; I believe God gave it to me in that moment, as I chose to obey.

The opposite of forgiveness is bitterness. When you let seeds of bitterness take root in your heart, your whole life becomes tainted. The bitterness you hold against one person soon spreads to others. You continue to collect offenses, seeing the worst in others, getting picky about little things, even plotting revenge. In such a case, you become the loser.

But Grace stands ready with open arms. All it takes to unleash it is one decision to give up your own way and choose God's way of forgiveness.

I guess the tears in that service were for me. I found myself amazed by the grace I could find . . . in heaven's eyes.

11

A

Contrite Spirit

During my growing-up years in Olney, Illinois, I went with other kids from our church to summer camp near Martinsville, Indiana. It was the typical rustic environment of trees and trails and bugs and practical jokes. You could join the "Sweat Hog Club" by getting up at 6:30 A.M. and running around the lake several times. Or you could join the "Polar Bear Club" by getting up in the same early chill and rolling off the edge into the swimming pool.

I had tons of fun doing skits and kayaking and even acquiring a boyfriend or two, as I recall. But there was time as well to think about important life issues.

One day during the morning session when we all gathered in the small chapel, the speaker talked about having "a contrite spirit." Although I'd heard that term once or twice in Bible readings, I didn't have a clue what it meant.

The man held up a saltine cracker. "See this cracker?" he said. "Okay—let's smash it a few times." With that, he laid it down on a table and pounded it repeatedly with his fist.

"We now have a *contrite* cracker," he explained. "It's

all in pieces; it's not together anymore. Its form, its stiffness has been broken. *Broken*—that's another word the Bible uses alongside *contrite*. The Lord wants us to be *broken* about our sin.

"The opposite of all this is to be *proud*. When I started here this morning, you could say I had a *proud* cracker. Now it's a broken and contrite one."

He then read some Scriptures:

> *The LORD is nigh unto them that are of a broken heart; and saveth such as be of a contrite spirit* (Psalm 34:18).

> *The sacrifices of God are a broken spirit: a broken and a contrite heart, O God, thou wilt not despise* (Psalm 51:17).

> *For thus saith the high and lofty One . . . I dwell in the high and holy place, with him also that is of a contrite and humble spirit, to revive the spirit of the humble, and to revive the heart of the contrite ones* (Isaiah 57:15).

> *For all those things hath mine hand made, and all those things have been, saith the LORD: but to this man will I look, even to him that is poor and of a contrite spirit, and trembleth at my word* (Isaiah 66:2, all verses from KJV).

Apparently, being contrite is a *good* thing as far as God is concerned. He welcomes the attitude of humility and brokenness. People who are rigid and self-composed do not gain his approval nearly as quickly as those who are pliable and receptive.

When God lets the circumstances of life make us contrite, we no longer "have it all together." Instead, the pieces of our lives are apart, open, vulnerable. This condition scares us to some degree; we sense the loss of composure. But from these pieces God can make what he wills.

When I was in the jungle, I thought more than once about Naomi, who with her family moved to a distant land (Moab) and then watched everything fall apart: her husband died and then both her sons. She summarized it to her daughters-in-law this way: "The LORD's hand has gone out against me!" (Ruth 1:13, NIV).

In my mind's eye, I could still see that camp speaker's hand coming down on that table years before. That's how I felt in captivity: like a cracker being crushed.

In reality, however, it was the Abu Sayyaf doing the beating, and God was simply allowing their efforts as part of a process to soften me toward him. I could do nothing to resist. I could only yield.

When things are not going well, we are humbled. We know we need outside help. It is in such conditions that "the LORD is nigh," as Psalm 34 (KJV) puts it. This is good for our spiritual well-being. We are reminded, as the saying goes, that God is God and we are not.

During the years we lived in Malaybalay, we had a Filipino friend whose husband was an alcoholic. For a while he would straighten up, and things would be fine. But then he would fall back into drinking, and the whole family would be in shambles.

This woman went to a friend of ours for counsel. "I'm at my wits' end," she cried. "I don't know what else to do with him. I give up."

The friend replied, "Praise the Lord!"

The woman looked up in shock. What an inappropriate remark to someone whose home life was awful.

"God has been waiting for you to do just that—to give up," the counselor explained. "He's been hoping you would stop worrying, stop badgering your husband, stop trying to fix this, and all the rest. He just wants you to acknowledge you can't handle this after all. Now is the time that God can work."

And as far as I know, the husband is doing fine today. When we moved away, the whole family was back in church, and the situation had stabilized. Both the marriage and the parenting had been rescued by surrender to a divine solution.

One of Martin's favorite books was entitled *Christ Esteem* by a Lutheran pastor and radio host named Don Matzat. Matzat talks at length about the current chase after self-esteem as the answer to our many difficulties and how just feeling better about ourselves doesn't solve the deep issues. He writes:

> The devil doesn't care how religious we are as long as we live for ourselves, remain consciously wrapped up in ourselves, try to feel good about ourselves, and cover up the nakedness of empty, meaningless

lives through a spiritual charade. Martin Luther
wrote concerning self-indulgence and human pride:
"Against this secret villain we must pray God daily
to suppress our self-esteem."

I'm sure the pop psychologists of our day would be
horrified by such a statement. But then, Martin Luther
wouldn't especially care.

Next in Matzat's book comes a section entitled "How
Badly Do You Hurt?"

There are many hurting, unhappy, discouraged
people in our world today. They struggle with their
little problems and failures, chasing after every
flimsy hope that is held out to them whereby they
might overcome and find relief from their personal
fears, broken hearts, worries, guilt, and feelings of
inadequacy. They buy self-help books, undergo
counseling, and seek to discover some gimmick,
some way of thinking or acting that will provide
relief.

If you are one of these hurting people, the question is: Are you hurting enough to give up on yourself? Are you unhappy enough and miserable
enough to turn away from yourself with all your
problems and failures and seek relief in a relationship with the person of Jesus Christ? Many claim to
be hurting but are really not hurting enough. . . .
Jesus is the answer and does provide help, relief,
comfort, peace, and joy, but surrendering and
giving up on self is a prerequisite. . . .

Are you willing to stop kicking? Are you willing to see all your little problems and unresolved conflicts, discouragements and disappointments, bad habits, negative attitudes, faults, and failures as being means whereby God is at work bringing you to the end of yourself? Are you willing to be nailed to the cross of Christ and buried in the waters of your baptism?[10]

When I got back to the States, I bought a stack of these books and gave them out as Christmas gifts that first year in honor of Martin, and also because I too believed the point being made. Only in Jesus do we find equilibrium and wholeness. Only he can make us competent. Without him, we can do nothing, as he reminded the disciples at the Last Supper. A broken and contrite spirit is what he sees as the starting point.

When we are weak, Christ has the opportunity to be strong. When we are shattered, he can then go to work reassembling us. When we are defeated, he lends us his victory. When we are dispirited, he infuses us with his joy.

Of course, we push mightily against the idea of being broken. We keep telling ourselves we are "okay" and even good. Politicians instinctively drone about "the goodness of the American people," even while asking for more funds to fight crime on our streets. The badness is always in somebody else, not us.

The Muslims with whom we lived for a year had a big problem with the Genesis story about Lot, the nephew of Abraham, committing incest with his two daughters. In their view of history, Lot is a "prophet" right alongside Noah, Moses, David, Isaiah, and the rest. (And it's true that Lot gets at least a partial compliment in the New Testament; see 2 Peter 2:7.)

"How could your Holy Book say such a horrible thing about a holy man?" they raved. They were sure that the tale of him fathering his own grandsons (Genesis 19:30-38) was invented by some Jew or Christian with abominable motives.

Martin's reply to our captors was, "You know, I guess that's a reminder of humanity's incredible sinfulness. We all make choices, even as Lot and his daughters did. And we're 100 percent responsible for what we choose. The amazing thing is that God has mercy on us; he's willing to make things right after we've really messed up."

The Bible says, "If we say we have no sin, we are only fooling ourselves and refusing to accept the truth. But if we confess our sins to him, he is faithful and just to forgive us and to cleanse us from every wrong" (1 John 1:8-9). This is yet another part of having a contrite spirit before God. It means we admit our faults and ask him to pardon us.

The same is true of our abilities and strengths. Even those need to be laid down before the only One who can purify our motives. Our career plans are bound to derail somewhere along the line unless they are submitted to the Lord, who holds all wisdom in his hand. He is in charge, and we must be his humble servants.

Paul said the whole treasure of the gospel had been placed "in jars of clay to show that this all-surpassing power is from God and not from us" (2 Corinthians 4:7, NIV). His metaphor was a reference to his very human self and those of his colleagues in the ministry. Clay pots are usually cheap. They break easily—perhaps not as easily as a cracker, but they are certainly not strong, as you will find out if you ever drop one on the ground. That is meant to be a picture of us, as it was of Paul. We are no big deal. We are vulnerable and replaceable. If others see God's powerful truth inside of us, they know right away where the value lies and where it doesn't.

When asked the frequent question, "How did you survive that whole year in captivity?" I find it hard to give a short answer. A part of it, I do know, is that Martin and I had made a life habit of saying, in response to whatever challenge, "Yes, Lord." Whenever the work of the mission posed a request to us, we tried to nod our heads affirmatively. That is what *servants* are supposed to do, correct? This helped us when the really dreadful ordeal began on May 27, 2001.

This certainly does not mean that this was our natural response or that we always *liked* what we had said yes to. Many times it was far from fun.

But in the end, the Master knows what he is doing. In my life and yours, he is pursuing a good plan. What he needs from us is willingness to follow.

12

Your
Survival Kit

I have a little rented storage unit over by the railroad tracks at the edge of Rose Hill. Slowly, as I have the time and emotional energy, I'm going through our belongings that came back from the Philippines.

The other day, I got into a box of Martin's stuff from the airplane hangar. His technical manuals, his books on flying in turbulence, his Bible study helps . . . they were all there.

What a treasure it was to come across his favorite CDs. There was *The Best of Collin Raye* and *George Winston Piano Solos* and *Acapella Hymns*. I set them aside to take home. I could listen to these while trying to go to sleep at night, and they would remind me of my wonderful husband.

Then I picked up something even more special: his survival kit that he always kept under the seat of his airplane. It was khaki-colored with zippers and pouches, sort of like a medium-sized fanny pack. Martin used to spend hours figuring out what he might need if he ever got stranded. He had turned the assembling of these items into a high science.

I started pulling them out, one by one:

- A small flashlight with two AA batteries
- A tiny strobe light to flash toward the sky if rescuers were looking for him
- Flares
- A compass
- A mirror
- A whistle
- A Cricket lighter
- Puritabs, to purify drinking water
- Advil, Tylenol, and mefenamic acid if the pain got really bad
- Band-Aids
- Disinfectant
- Vicks VapoRub
- An antihistamine
- Maalox

By now I was sobbing. "Oh, Martin," I said, "you had everything right here! If only we'd had this for the year in the jungle. But we never got to use it."

I kept going.

- Off! spray, to repel insects
- Soap
- Contact lens solution
- Toilet paper
- Shampoo
- A toothbrush
- Coffee mix
- Orange juice mix
- Cream of chicken soup mix

- A tiny tin can for heating water over a fire
- Salt and pepper
- Sugar and creamer
- Raisins
- Mints
- Candles and matches
- An emergency blanket he had found in an army
  surplus store. It was actually a big piece of thin
  aluminum-laminated polyethylene, 84 inches by 54
  inches—but folded down to the size of a postcard! He
  was so proud of that find.
- Blue nylon string
- Finally, his Pilots for Christ edition of the New
  Testament

All this was carefully crammed into the survival kit. I stared at the items in wonder. When I tried to put them all back inside, I couldn't get even close. Martin was a master packer, whether loading cargo into his airplane or small stuff into his survival kit.

The Bible says that "as we know Jesus better, his divine power gives us *everything we need* for living a godly life. He has called us to receive his own glory and goodness! And by that same mighty power, *he has given us all of his rich and wonderful promises.* He has promised that you will escape the decadence all around you caused by evil desires and that you will share in his divine nature" (2 Peter 1:3-4, italics added).

We are the recipients of a spiritual survival kit that includes everything we require. Whatever the threat or complication, we have what we need to cope. It's not miles away on a distant shelf, or in a pharmacy; it is already within us, just waiting to be opened and put to use.

I know that we often don't feel equipped. We look at the challenges in our life and think we are empty-handed. But we are not. The Word of God assures us that we can manage the situation after all. Through the "rich and wonderful promises" we are outfitted to go forward and overcome.

In Martin's Bible I found a three-by-five card from a time he spoke on a Sunday morning in Aritao. It was this Scripture from 1 Corinthians 1:8-9 (NIV):

He will keep you strong to the end, so that you will be blameless on the day of our Lord Jesus Christ. God, who has called you . . . is faithful.

That card now rides around in my Bible instead of Martin's. It tells me to keep going when my life is hard. It reminds me to draw upon God's strength. It assures me that his provision is adequate. It promises me that I can make it after all. I can survive.

God does not mean for us to be cowed by our circumstances, even though we often are. He means for us to keep our balance and rise to meet the challenge through his enabling power.

We are not the first to do this, of course. We are simply following the precedent of "a great High Priest who has gone to heaven, Jesus the Son of God. Let us cling to him and never stop trusting him. This High Priest of ours understands our weaknesses, for he faced all of the same temptations we do, yet he did not sin. So let us come boldly to the throne of our gracious God. There we will receive his mercy, and we will find grace to help us when we need it" (Hebrews 4:14-16).

Prayer, I think, is not our effort to get God's attention. We are already, at all times, in his line of sight. We can therefore "come boldly" in search of his mercy, grace, and strength. Too often our praying is framed as trying to get God to do something, when he has already done everything. He has blessed us with every spiritual blessing. He has equipped us for every challenge.

Now, we must simply use what he has given us to get through today's gauntlet. He will give us well-timed help just when we need it. We are pursuing *his* mission with *his* resources.

My oldest, Jeff, is already hot on the trail of becoming a pilot like his father. In fact, Martin had promised to teach him to fly when he turned fifteen. Jeff was fourteen when we were captured, and so that never happened. But now, back in the States, he has been able to pursue his dream regardless.

As for me, I'm being stretched just letting Jeffrey *drive*, let alone fly! Whenever he is at the wheel, I'm a typical badgering mother: "Isn't this a forty-mile-an-hour zone?" . . . "Jeff, you're tailgating; don't be so close to this guy in front of you" . . . all the usual stuff. He just rolls his eyes and sighs.

It is definitely a good thing I'm not in the cockpit with him. His flight instructor, meanwhile, says he's doing fine. Armed with his student pilot certificate, Jeff recently made his first cross-country solo flight. The day before, his instructor went with him as Jeff flew from here to Chanute in southeastern Kansas, then on to Bartlesville, Oklahoma, and home again. All the necessary instructions were covered.

The next day, the weather was perfect, and so—even though it was a school day—I allowed him to skip classes and attempt his solo flight over the same route. The winds aloft weren't bad (which is a minor miracle in Kansas). I drove him to the airport, where he filed his flight plan and then went out onto the ramp to check his plane. I stood there shivering in the cold as he did his work, thinking, *Oh, how I remember doing this with*

Martin! My ears were about to freeze off when Jeff finally lifted into the air and disappeared to the east.

I knew I had about three hours to go home and do things on my list before heading back to the airport to see him return. One of them was to catch up on e-mails. To a New Tribes Mission friend I wrote, "You know, right now as I'm writing to you, Jeff is flying alone for the first time. . . ."

And then the thought came to me: *No—Jeff's not flying alone. The Lord is with him. Martin never flew alone, remember? The Lord was with him, too. Like father, like son, okay?*

Sure enough, Jeff arrived back in fine shape. In fact, he landed early; I missed it. He was all smiles as he walked into the terminal. "That was fun," he said. We talked about his takeoffs and landings, and then as we headed out the door, he added, "Could we stop and cele-brate on the way home?" Indeed we did, at Sonic for burgers.

"Be strong and courageous," Moses told the Israelites. "Do not be afraid or terrified . . . for the LORD your God goes with you; he will never leave you nor forsake you" (Deuteronomy 31:6, NIV). I choose to believe that God meant exactly that. We are never abandoned. We travel through life with the survival kit of God's grace.

13

Flashbacks
of
Gratitude

Sometimes you have more reasons to give thanks than you think you do. When everything is going downhill, your mind is not exactly attuned to the positive. The hard times, however, lend fresh perspective to normal living.

I was grateful, of course, when the community of Rose Hill volunteered to build a new house for my kids and me. This was an awesome gift, as we were trying to get back on our feet in those early months.

As word spread through *USA Today*, *Guideposts*, and other media, people around the country began chipping in to help. One day a man from Oak Express showed up at the house we were using temporarily. He left his card and said his company wanted to furnish our entire place!

I thought, *He obviously doesn't know how big this new house is going to be.* But when I called to get more information, the offer proved to be genuine. One day the kids and I drove to Wichita and walked through the store, picking out what we wanted. Today our home is a showcase of lovely light oak furniture. For my bedroom, which is small, I chose a unique all-in-one bed with a nice headboard and drawers underneath for storage, three on each side. That way I made the most of the space.

But even small things can trigger a spurt of gratitude. One night as I was sleeping in that handsome bed, I sort of came half-awake . . . the house was silent . . . the clock said 2:30 . . . and I realized something odd: *I'm sleeping on my stomach!*

What is so strange about that, you ask? Well, when I shared a single hammock with my husband for nearly nine months under the open sky in the jungle, turning onto my stomach was clearly impossible. If I tried it, I'd promptly flip myself or Martin out onto the hard ground. The only way I could manage was to lie carefully on my back or my side, with my head tucked into his ankles, while his head was at the other end of the hammock near my feet. And once the two of us got into place, that was it—we stayed put for the night, because there was no room to fidget or adjust.

Now lying in a spacious bed with freedom to take any posture I pleased, I was caught up in a moment of worship. *Oh, Lord,* I said, *thank you that I can lie on my stomach!* An eccentric praise, I admit, but it was entirely justified in my case. I had come to appreciate certain things most Americans don't notice.

Don't get me wrong: I would still rather be shivering in a hammock getting poked by Martin's kneecaps than to have this nice warm bed all to myself. But since that is no longer available to me, I gladly accept the spacious provision—and give thanks.

➤<

On another day I was driving and thought about how nice it is to have left-turn lanes. What a concept—a whole space designated for people turning left so that everyone else can get on their way faster. And the drivers (at least most of them) respect that designation and don't clog up the left-turn lane unless they're really turning left!

In a country such as the Philippines, that wouldn't work. Drivers are too accustomed to flowing like amoeba in a stream, filling up every open space the instant it appears in an effort to get ahead. That's why emergency vehicles have such a hard time getting to accidents. The idea of pulling over to the side and letting the ambulance through is considered peculiar.

"Isn't it great to have these lanes for turning left?" I exclaimed one day when the kids and I were driving somewhere. They looked at me, totally mystified. Oh, well, moms are allowed to say ridiculous things, aren't they?

Since coming back to America, I have walked down a sidewalk and marveled at its smoothness. There's no need to keep an eye out for stones, roots, and other hazards because straight, level concrete supports my steps.

I'm not saying that we in this country should feel superior because of our various advancements in efficiency or convenience. Lots of things in life are more important than traffic management. I'm just saying that when you have lived without these things for sixteen years, you notice them afresh, and you appreciate them more.

>*<

A few years after returning to the States, I am no longer awestruck by conveniences such as oak beds and left-turn lanes. Still, I can't predict when something will trigger a memory.

One day I was waiting at the middle school for Mindy to come out of the locker room after her basketball game. Presently she appeared with her assortment of stuff: a backpack full of books, her gym bag with shoes and other gear, her water bottle.

"Mom, can you help me get all this to the car?" she asked.

I picked up the backpack and slung it over one shoulder as we headed out the door, down the sidewalk, and toward the parking lot maybe a hundred yards away. The weight of the books bore down upon me . . . and suddenly, I had a vivid flashback. I was no longer crossing a school yard in Kansas; I was on Basilan Island getting ready to haul a backpack through the jungle for the next eight or ten hours. The physical sensation of that load on my shoulder brought it all back.

I calmed myself and took a deep breath. I said nothing to Mindy. Inside, however, I thought, *You know, I don't have to carry this thing up and down mountains all day. I only have to carry it as far as that van over there. Thank you, Lord.* We made our way to the parking lot and I began to drive us home.

On the road, however, I had a second thought.

A long time ago a Man carried my heavy load up a steep

hill. It was far more than a backpack. It was the weight of my sin.

I will be forever grateful for what Jesus did for me that day at Calvary, and for us all. "He personally carried away our sins in his own body on the cross so we can be dead to sin and live for what is right" (1 Peter 2:24).

In fact, only sinners qualify for this wonderful gift. The prophet Isaiah explained that "The LORD is not too weak to save you, and he is not becoming deaf. He can hear you when you call. But there is a problem—your sins have cut you off from God" (59:1-2). The good news from Jesus is that he resolved this problem for us.

I am told that in Chinese script, the pictograph for righteousness is formed by placing the character of a lamb above the pronoun *I*. What an appropriate symbol. Jesus was "the Lamb of God who takes away the sin of the world" (John 1:29). Christ is our answer. We make the ultimate trade-off when we accept him as our Savior. We trade our sin for his righteousness.

What a special privilege to become God's child. How amazing it is to have our sins forgiven and begin walking with God each day. I can think of no higher reason to be grateful.

14

*Am I
Accomplishing
Anything?*

Late at night on December 30, 2003, I was sitting on the couch in my living room thinking about the year wrapping up. The kids were already in bed, the Christmas tree was still glowing in the corner, and the gas fireplace was burning. I had been home from the Philippines for a little more than eighteen months. What had I accomplished in that length of time?

I started telling myself . . .

Gracia, you're not spending enough time speaking to groups. You need to be out telling your story. Invitations to churches and other audiences were indeed plentiful.

Gracia, this foundation of yours [which was started to channel money toward mission aviation, tribal mission work, and ministry to Muslims] *would really be going places if you'd just put some energy into it.* The Christian Community Foundation in Kansas City had done all the legwork, but the public voice for my foundation had to be mine.

Gracia, you're too busy. The kids really need you in these important years. Certainly. Jeff was already a junior in high school, while Mindy was in eighth grade, and Zach in seventh.

My thoughts wandered to a certain individual in my life. A month or two before, I had promised myself, *Okay, I am definitely not going to have any more conflict with so-and-so. I will handle this smoothly from here on.* But, in fact, tension had raised its head again.

Before long I was overwhelmed with the list of what I *should* be doing. If you are like me, it's easy to get down on yourself for what you haven't done. You look at your recent past, and you see one gaping hole after another. You should have taken care of this, and that, and the other . . . but you didn't. You start to feel like a total waste. Life, once again, is out of control. You are spinning your wheels, going nowhere.

This makes you feel inferior. Your overall impression of yourself plunges. You are just taking up space, consuming food and money, but not making a contribution to your family, your church, your community, your world. A heaviness hangs over your spirit.

For most of us, achievement and the affirmation of others are linked to value. If we don't feel we are accomplishing much, we assume we're not *worth* much. A lot of women who are at home full-time accept this equation. In a different sense, so do a considerable number of men and women who look at their job performance and wince. Doing becomes a measure of being.

What we forget is that God made us with innate value, before we ever did a single thing to prove it. The theologians call this *positional truth*. Once we have received entrance into God's family, we are totally acceptable to him, even loved by him. We have the right to come boldly into his presence. We have been given eternal life. All of that makes us valuable.

Dozens of times in the New Testament letters we find this somewhat odd phrase: to be "in Christ." It cannot mean a literal insertion into his physical body, of course, like you would say you're living "in Pennsylvania" or swimming "in the lake." It is a metaphor, but a very powerful one, for being enveloped in the essence of Christ and thereby endowed with his attributes. To be "in Christ" includes:

- being alive to God (Romans 6:11)
- being without condemnation (Romans 8:1)
- being loved (Romans 8:39)
- being eligible for resurrection (1 Corinthians 15:22)
- being established (2 Corinthians 1:21)
- being triumphant (2 Corinthians 2:14)
- being a new creation (2 Corinthians 5:17)
- being free (Galatians 2:4)
- being reconciled with people who are not like you (Ephesians 2:13; 3:6)
- being encouraged and consoled (Philippians 2:1)
- being confident (1 Timothy 3:13)
- in fact . . . having "every good thing" (Philemon 6, NIV)

These and many more blessings are ours as a result of our association with Christ. They are valuable in their own right. And they set us up to be high achievers in our world. From this base comes the strength to go out into life and be productive.

I frequently get letters from those who read my first book, *In the Presence of My Enemies*. Not a few of these come from inmates. Having lots of time on their hands, they often write pages of information about themselves, how they are praying for me, when their release date is, and what they hope to do once they get out.

One letter that particularly touched my heart was from a man who had been convicted of molesting a child. He vigorously defended his innocence. I didn't form any conclusion regarding that, but I did write back to him the following:

> Your situation sounds very sad and hopeless. But that is exactly the kind of situation that God specializes in. Making good come out of hopelessness—it's not even hard for him. So you can be encouraged.
>
> Paul the apostle declared: "I can do all things through Christ who strengthens me" [see Philippians 4:13, NKJV]. The amazing thing is that he wrote these words while he was in prison! He wasn't going anywhere. In fact, he was chained twenty-four hours a day. I know how disheartening that can be, because my husband, Martin, had that happen to him. It's depressing and degrading.

What was Paul even talking about? He couldn't do anything; he was a prisoner.

I believe the sentence is saying that he could do what he knew he should do, which was to rise above the situation . . . beat the depression . . . not lose heart . . . forgive the creeps who had put him behind bars . . . and stay faithful to the One who gave his life to ransom him from sin.

If Paul affirmed that he could "do all things" inside a prison cell because of the presence of Christ, our situations are not that impossible. We too can overcome the difficulties, the irritations, and even the inertia that try to immobilize us. We are sons and daughters of the King of kings.

Just because our value is already established in Christ doesn't mean that we sit back and cease being productive. Instead, we recognize that the key to a Christian's accomplishment is only partly a matter of diligence and initiative and hard work. It is also a matter of being grounded in Christ, of attempting each task "with the help of Christ who gives me the strength I need" (Philippians 4:13). This is how we truly achieve.

It was good on that New Year's week that I reached for a nearby photo album. I began turning the pages, which reminded me of at least a few things I *had* accomplished during 2003. We'd been able to move into this house, for one. A year before, the house hadn't even been finished.

We had made it through Jeff's emergency appendectomy, and he was in good health again.

We had cleaned out our garage. (For some readers, that won't sound like much, I know. But the rest of you will understand the magnitude of the challenge.) We had also begun sorting out the things that had been shipped back from the Philippines.

My correspondence was in better shape. A year before, I had college girls who were home on holiday break scribbling letters for me and running to the post office (as well as buying groceries when I was too swamped to do so). Now I had a regular part-time secretary working in a little downstairs room of my house that had become an office.

I certainly had not achieved everything during the year that I had wanted to do or that needed to be done. But at least some things got handled. It was good for me to be reminded of them.

Even as we rest in the inherent worth that God has given us, we know that someday we will all stand before the Lord for a review of our accomplishments. I think the review will probably be both quantitative (how many things we got done) and qualitative (how well we did them). The Lord will no doubt also ask whether those things were important or trivial. Did our accomplishments matter in the eternal sense?

I hope to give a good account of myself on that day. I certainly will not have achieved everything I hoped to or could have. I know there will be embarrassing gaps. But as I live these years with my feet firmly anchored in Christ, I will achieve more than I ever could otherwise. I can face him with confidence and peace.

15

*What
Role for Praise?*

Relax: This is not going to be one of those glib and superficial pep talks that says, "Just praise the Lord, and all your problems will melt away!" When life spins out of control, it takes more than a few magic words to stabilize the situation.

If we truly believe that God is real, however—that he is good-hearted and loving and mindful of our trial— those facts endure apart from what we are going through. Whether the sun is shining on our circumstances or not, whether everybody likes us or hates us, whether we have plenty of food and money or none at all—God is still God. He never changes.

The bedrock fact that he is always "on duty" is of tremendous value. You may feel like thanking him for that anchorage in your otherwise storm-tossed life. In so doing, you participate in *praise*.

One of the oddest things that happened to Martin and me in the jungle occurred the day our group was on the trail and stopped to rest at a little farmhouse. The occupants had fled, as was common. The Abu Sayyaf rushed us inside so that any civilians who might come along wouldn't see us. Meanwhile, our captors started fires for cooking rice and sat around talking outside.

All of a sudden as we waited, through the bamboo walls we heard someone humming a verse of "How Great Thou Art"! Martin and I looked at each other in amazement. The song kept going for a while, and then faded away.

We could not resist the urge to finish the song very quietly: "Then sings my soul, my Savior God to thee: How great thou art, how great thou art. . . ."[11]

I doubt that the captors outside heard us. Nothing was ever said. But in our hearts, we were truly worshiping right there in the jungle. We were reminded of God's greatness—which had not diminished at all despite our circumstances.

"How in the world does a Muslim know that song?" I asked when we finished.

Martin reminded me that Christian missionaries had worked for many years even here in the southern Philippines, sharing the gospel and planting churches. Mindanao and the smaller islands were especially influenced by the Christian and Missionary Alliance denomination. Some of the Abu Sayyaf, they had told us, had attended C&MA churches when they were younger. Even though the siren call of militant Islam had eventually pulled them away, they still remembered some of the music.

"How Great Thou Art" became, in some ways, our anthem as hostages. I told in my first book about teaching Angie the words so she and Fe and I could sing it as a trio.

Its words in the second verse, "When through the woods and forest glades I wander," were especially apropos.

Martin would listen and then say to me, "You know, Gracia, maybe God has us here simply to praise him in this dark place."

The book of Acts tells about a dreadful night that Paul and Silas spent in prison in Philippi. They had tried to bring the light of the gospel to this "major city of the district of Macedonia and a Roman colony" (Acts 16:12). When they confronted the power of demons in a young slave girl and set her free through the superior power of God, the town went crazy. Paul and Silas were promptly dragged before a judge, who had them stripped of their clothing, severely beaten, and thrown into the maximum-security ward of the city jail.

I'm sure you know the story of what happened a few hours later. Instead of sinking into self-pity and depression or fuming with rage about the blatant injustice they had suffered, the two men began "praying and singing hymns to God" (Acts 16:25). They released the power of musical praise in the middle of a dark night. They affirmed what they knew to be true, despite all indications to the contrary.

And God showed up! A strong earthquake rattled the city at just that moment. The prison building heaved and shuddered. Its doors swung open. The chains that anchored Paul and Silas to the wall clattered loose. Incarceration became emancipation in a matter of seconds.

The whole situation changed dramatically. The warden, fearing that he would be blamed for all the chaos, came close to committing suicide, until Paul stopped him. Before the sun came up the next morning, the man "and his entire household rejoiced because they all believed in God" (Acts 16:34). A few hours later, the court officials were embarrassedly coaxing the two missionaries to step out into the sunshine and go on their way.

I am not claiming that the praise of Paul and Silas directly triggered the earthquake. But I do believe it is fair to say that affirming the goodness and power of God is always appropriate. It tells God that we have not lost our bearings. We still know who is ultimately in charge of the world. And we invite his intervention in the midst of our trauma.

When stress arises in our life, I can think of nothing better than to praise the Lord for his reliability, for his strength, for his ability to work on our behalf. This is not manipulation; this is just stating the facts. Don't be surprised if he shows up in your personal prison to start throwing timbers around and snapping leg-irons open. He is, after all, the God of "Let my people go!" Freedom is a part of his nature.

I love the perspective of King Jehoshaphat when he was threatened by a massive coalition of invading armies in the 850s B.C. He was in a terrible jam. The clouds of war were thundering overhead. In front of the entire nation,

he prayed aloud, "We do not know what to do, but our
eyes are upon you" (2 Chronicles 20:12, NIV).

That sense of focus on the Lord instead of the environment evoked a dramatic prophecy from a Levite
named Jahaziel, encouraging everyone who heard it.
Early the next morning, the king embarked on the
strangest, most upside-down tactical strategy in the
annals of warfare.

> *The king appointed singers to walk ahead of the army,*
> *singing to the LORD and praising him for his holy*
> *splendor. This is what they sang:*
> *"Give thanks to the LORD;*
> *his faithful love endures forever!"*
>
> (2 Chronicles 20:21)

As you read this story, you are certain that the next
thing that happened was an awful bloodbath. Surely the
floating melodies of the vanguard singers were about to
turn into screams of agony as the enemy swords flashed
and slashed in the sunlight.

But that is not what occurred.

Inexplicably, the opposing armies began fighting
among themselves. One faction took on another, while
the third faction jumped on both of them. By the time
Jehoshaphat's "choir" and infantry got to an overlook
point in the terrain, "there were dead bodies lying on
the ground for as far as they could see. Not a single one
of the enemy had escaped" (2 Chronicles 20:24). There
was no battle left for the Israelites to fight.

I don't understand that at all. It defies all military logic. It is definitely a "God thing." It shows the almighty Lord intervening on behalf of those who concentrate on him and his mighty character.

The valley where they collected all the plunder—a job that required three days—received a new name that week. On maps of the Holy Land it became known as the Valley of Beracah, a Hebrew word that means "blessing" or "praise." With a different strategy, this could have become a valley of slaughter. The exaltation of God made all the difference.

In the battles of our life, when we face overwhelming threats to life and limb, it is always good to praise the Lord. It states a higher reality than what we see with our natural eyes. It affirms our place in the hands of a loving and strong heavenly Father, who will never stop caring about our welfare. He is, indeed, worthy of every accolade we can offer, whether circumstances seem to agree or not.

When Martin and I were in the jungle, we would occasionally pray in the mornings, "God, could you do something special for us today, just to let us know that you haven't forgotten us? We're still here in the awful situation—how about encouraging us with something little? We need to know if we're still on your radar screen."

And then we would wait to see if anything unusual would happen.

I remember that one day, after such a prayer, an Abu Sayyaf member gave us a Coca-Cola! In this remote tangle of trees and vines and insects, far from civilization, a can with the familiar red label was suddenly dropped into our laps. Actually, the miracle was not so much that a pack of Cokes had arrived in the camp as that the guys didn't gulp them all down themselves. On this particular day, they actually gave one to the Americans!

As we popped open the top, we quietly breathed, "Thank you, Lord. You remembered us, didn't you! For this small token of your care, we give you thanks."

Whether in small ways or large, by subtle means or dramatic ones, God's love for his children shows through.

16

*The Power
of a Gentle Word*

Many tense situations are made worse when we launch an inflammatory comment or lash out at an opponent in a way that riles the ego and fires the emotions. Before long, a shouting match is underway. Far better to hold our tongue and say nothing.

But we can do something even better: We can speak a word of peace and kindness in the face-off. This achieves more than just a cool détente; it opens the road to healing and warmth.

I had the immeasurable blessing of being married for nineteen years to a man whose words were consistently gentle, temperate, and uplifting. Whether speaking to me, to the children, to our American supporters, or to Filipino villagers, Martin was the essence of verbal grace.

In the mountains of Mindanao is a smattering of tribal villages where our Australian missionary colleagues Paul and Deb had settled and built an airstrip. Martin flew there often to take them supplies, carry out people who needed a doctor, and just encourage Paul and Deb in their work.

Not far away was another village where a man named Pik-Pik lived. He was a gambler, a heavy drinker, and a frequent fighter. His reputation for having a hot temper was well known in the village.

Some of his relatives and friends began walking over to the first village each week to attend the Bible studies that the missionaries were leading. This irritated Pik-Pik, and he said so bluntly. "You're just wasting your time," he told them.

He also noticed that whenever he heard the sound of Martin's Cessna 180 coming in for a landing, people dropped everything and went running to the airstrip. "Why do you act so excited when the plane comes?" he carped. "It's not as if it's coming for you. You don't even get to talk to the pilot—why would he ever want to talk to you?"

"No, no, you're wrong," his relatives said. "The pilot's name is Martin, and he is our brother. He has even flown some of our people to the hospital in Cagayan."

Pik-Pik was not impressed. But one day when he heard the engine drone, he elected to walk over to the hillside airstrip and see for himself what the fuss was about. He stood not at the top like everyone else but at the lower end, smack in the center of the approach.

People began yelling and waving for him to get out of the way as Martin made his final descent. He wouldn't budge.

Martin set the plane down without hitting Pik-Pik, fortunately. He taxied up to the crowd, got out of the cockpit, took off his sunglasses, and greeted everyone warmly. Then he took a walk down to the end of the strip for a friendly conversation with Pik-Pik. He laughed as he put his hand on the Filipino's shoulder and explained the necessity of keeping the approach clear whenever a plane was landing.

The man was surprised not to get chewed out by the pilot. Martin's manner was disarming. Shortly after that, Pik-Pik began showing up for some of the Bible teachings.

By the next year, he had made his personal commitment to Jesus Christ. Just over a year after that, he started an outreach in a third village, where today there are some forty believers. A young man named Rodil from that little group is now a ministry associate of the missionaries, working with yet another nearby church, which has 120 members. In early 2003 Rodil married a young woman named Annie, who had come to Christ in that church.

As for Pik-Pik, he is today an elder in the church in his home village, still faithfully following Christ. His negativity and suspicion are gone. He continues to impact the lives of others for good. The chain continues—all because a man put his hand on Pik-Pik's shoulder one day and treated him with gentleness.

I tell that story for the purpose of spotlighting a character trait that I believe made a huge difference in our year of captivity. When we were whisked away on the speedboat that fateful morning by a band of vicious terrorists, Martin's graciousness did not change. Soon he was showing our captors how to set the watches and operate the camcorders they had stolen from our group. He smiled as he put four D-cell batteries in a row to recharge the fading satellite phone they wanted to use to call their comrades on shore. As the days and weeks wore on, he would sit with the guys and chat: "Which is your home province? What does your father do? Is your mother in good health?"

One young captor said he wanted to become a mechanic someday. Martin spent hours with him explaining how internal-combustion engines work and drawing sketches on bits of paper.

Another wanted to learn English. Martin became his tutor.

They all were curious about American dating customs, and whether boys and girls really find each other the way they'd seen in Hollywood movies. Again, Martin explained patiently, with a smile.

These days interviewers often ask me, somewhat nervously, "During the year, did the Abu Sayyaf ever, uh, abuse you as a woman?" I reply that no, I was spared from that particular horror. All five of the other female hostages who were held longer than a few weeks were eventually sabayaed—taken as "booty of war" by one or another of the warriors and forced to share his hammock. I alone was left unmolested.

Why? It was not that I was American whereas the others were Filipino; indeed, the captors showed no mercy whatsoever to our fellow American, Guillermo Sobero. They brutally beheaded him. It was not that I somehow fast-talked my way out of their evil schemes. I couldn't even speak more than a few words in their various dialects.

Rather, I believe it was because I was the wife of that notably kind man. The terrorists genuinely liked Martin. They appreciated his generous spirit. They noted the soft twinkle in his eye, the caring words on his lips, and they could not bring themselves to violate his most cherished possession. When evening fell, they chained him to a tree but then left the two of us alone to rest together.

This is not to say that Martin had fallen into what psychologists call the Stockholm Syndrome, the propensity of hostages gradually to take their captors' side, to embrace the twisted causes of those who are, after all, feeding and sheltering them day after day. Martin never approved of jihad; he never tilted in favor of the Abu Sayyaf's radical agenda. In fact, he said to the leaders more than once, "Well, you know that I think what you're doing is morally wrong."

Martin rather gave evidence of what I might term the Jesus Syndrome: to walk through the midst of a cruel situation with poise and self-control, saying only what would edify and build up. He was able somehow to bless those who meant us harm—not just as a verbal pleasantry (the quick "God bless you" we often hear from entertainers and politicians) but in real and practical terms that left a lasting impact.

The Bible records this detail about Jesus early in his public ministry, "All who were there spoke well of him and were amazed by the gracious words that fell from his lips" (Luke 4:22). Even at the end, when vigilantes came to arrest him at night in the garden, Jesus kept a clear head and asked, "Whom are you looking for?" When they said they'd come for Jesus of Nazareth, he calmly replied, "I am he." And these tough, murderous thugs "all fell backward to the ground!" (John 18:4-6). They didn't know how to handle such calm in a man who obviously knew they had come to kill him.

The power of a gracious word is one of the mightiest forces in the universe.

When I speak to audiences these days, I frequently conclude with an old poem by Annie Johnson Flint (1866–1932) to highlight this theme. The literary style may evoke an earlier era, I know, but the message is for our time as well. God is looking for people to raise his gentle light in a foggy world. The poem says it this way:

> *His lamp am I, to shine where He shall say,*
> *And lamps are not for sunny rooms,*
> *Nor for the light of day;*
> *But for dark places of the earth,*
> *Where shame and crime and wrong have birth;*
> *Or for the murky twilight gray*
> *Where wandering sheep have gone astray;*
> *Or where the light of faith grows dim,*
> *And souls are groping after Him.*
> *And as sometimes a flame we find,*
> *Clear shining through the night,*

So bright we do not see the lamp,
But only see the light:
So may I shine—His light the flame,
That men may glorify His name.[12]

During all our years of service in the Philippines, Martin and I never thought of ourselves as "the real missionaries." We didn't live in the midst of any tribe, learn their language, translate the Bible, or set up churches. Martin always said, "Hey, I'm just the driver. I move stuff around so the real missionaries can do their job."

And yet . . . God used him to reach Pik-Pik and who knows how many others. God's work does not depend upon superstars. When ordinary people offer their heart and hands and speech to the Master, he accomplishes more through them than anyone would predict.

17

The Long Road to Joy

Could it have been any worse? On top of the all-night marches through the jungle, the skimpy food, the seventeen terrifying gun battles, the absence of all privacy, the lack of toiletry items, the blackout of information from the outside world, the constant filth, the daily disregard for one's person and values . . . was this as bad as it gets?

I appreciate the perspective of Matthew Henry, the godly English pastor and devotional writer who lived some three hundred years ago. One day while traveling from one town to another, he was beset by a band of highwaymen who mugged him and took all his money. In his journal that night, he wrote:

> *Let me be thankful, first, because I was never robbed before;*
> *Second, because though they took my purse, they did not take my life;*
> *Third, though they took my all, it was not very much;*
> *Fourth, that it was I who was robbed and not I who robbed.*

Well, that's a mature way to look at atrocity. I suppose I could say in a parallel vein that at least I had never been taken hostage before . . . I did escape with my life

. . . and I was not the terrorist but instead the one who was terrorized.

On a practical level: Yes, I suppose it could have been worse. For example, what if I had been pregnant? The added burden, both physical and emotional, would have taxed me perhaps to the breaking point. One of the hostages who was forced to become the mistress of group leader Janjalani declared at one point that she was pregnant. That was enough for even the hard-hearted Abu Sayyaf to release her.

Jesus, in his discourse about the future, spoke about a coming time when Jerusalem would be surrounded by armies, and the residents would need to run for their life. "How terrible it will be for pregnant women and for mothers nursing their babies. For there will be great distress in the land and wrath upon this people" he said in Luke 21:23. Any woman can imagine the feeling of running along the rough roads, gasping for breath, dragging children and a few belongings, heart pounding in her chest.

When our Lord spoke those words, I can't help wondering if, in the back of his mind, he was thinking of his own mother, Mary, who had made a torturous eighty-mile journey from Nazareth to Bethlehem during her ninth month of pregnancy. Any of us who have borne children will groan at the thought. The traditional paintings show the young Mary riding across the plains on a plodding, thump-thump-thumping donkey . . . ouch. But in fact, neither of the Gospel writers who tell the Nativity story (Matthew and Luke) says a single word about a donkey. This is pure embellishment in our imaginations. For all we know, Mary may have *walked* the entire distance alongside Joseph. The trip would have taken at least four days, if not longer . . . all to comply with the bureaucratic demand of a faraway Caesar who had picked this month, of all months, to conduct a census.

And yet, on a whole higher level, God was about the business of doing something magnificent. A few hours after the baby's delivery, an angel showed up to tell the shepherds, "I bring you good news of great joy for everyone!" (Luke 2:10). Joy? In the wake of utter exhaustion? After everything that could go wrong had gone wrong, from travel timing to lodging problems? Mary quite possibly knew not a soul in this strange town of Bethlehem, let alone a knowledgeable midwife; this was, after all, Joseph's home turf rather than hers. She had gone through one of the deepest valleys a woman can cross with hardly a friend to hold her hand.

I remember times in the jungle when I said to Martin, especially in the later months after many of the other female hostages had been ransomed, "I just need another woman to talk to. Don't be offended; I know you're doing your best to help me and lift my spirits. But I'm surrounded by *men*. I need a woman friend."

Mary had none, so far as we know. Even the infant she delivered was a boy.

And this was an occasion for joy?

The following week, Mary and Joseph went to the Temple in Jerusalem a few miles away for ceremonial

requirements. There an aged man of God named Simeon
noticed them. In his comments to Mary, he said specifi-
cally, "This child . . . will be the greatest *joy* to many"
(Luke 2:34, italics added).

At times, it is hard to see cause for joy in our life.
When circumstances have conspired to wear us down, to
drain our patience, to dash our hopes and dreams, we
feel within us the very opposite of joy. We are frustrated,
depressed, and even sometimes resentful.

Only the long perspective, the divine perspective, can
bring back the joy to our heart. Only when we remind
ourselves that "God is for us" (Romans 8:31), never
against us, can we rise above our immediate feelings.
The fact that we celebrate Christmas as a season of "joy
to the world" is because we now have the big picture.
We see what God was up to all along. Out of confusion
and distress he has brought salvation and hope.

Martin was always the one who handled the outdoor
Christmas decorations in our family. He had the
know-how and the patience to string lights along the
eaves and make our house attractive. Once I became a
single parent, I knew this just wasn't going to happen
anymore.

A few months after I got home from captivity, my
daughter, Mindy, my mother-in-law, and I went one
Saturday to the annual craft fair in Hillsboro, Kansas, a
town about sixty miles north of where we live. It's a
festive time; they block off the downtown streets so

people from all over the United States can display and sell their handiwork. Alongside the tables, there are food stands as well: funnel cakes and caramel apples, pies and chowder being sold by church groups . . . it's a delightful atmosphere.

Strolling along through the crowds, I spotted a set of oversize wooden letters—J, O, Y—painted red with aluminum anchor posts attached to the back so that they could be pushed into the ground of the front yard at Christmastime. The letters were nearly three feet tall. The O had a silhouette in the middle showing Joseph and Mary leaning over the baby Jesus.

I looked at the letters and thought, *Surely I can handle this.* I would rig up a spotlight in the grass to draw attention to the letters in the long December evenings. So I bought the set and took them home.

After Thanksgiving, when Mindy and I went out in the yard to place our display, we soon found that the winter ground was hard as a rock. We couldn't begin to push the aluminum rods down into the soil. Even this "simple" Christmas decoration was not going to be simple for us.

We got out a water hose and began soaking the ground, until it softened enough to let us anchor the three letters. We set up the spotlight with an extension cord from the garage and then went inside, proud of our success.

Within a day or two, people in Rose Hill began commenting when I'd see them in the post office, the grocery store, or Pizza Hut. "Gracia, I just love what you did to your house! There's this shadow of *joy* all over the front—it's so striking." I didn't quite know what they were talking about, until I went out to the street that night to take a look from a distance.

The spotlight sitting down on the grass was throwing a huge image of J-O-Y onto the front wall. It was the coolest thing. The silhouette of the Holy Family, in fact, was centered right on Zachary's bedroom. When I went inside to look at Zach's window, the part I could see was of Joseph bowing in prayer over the Child. How appropriate for my fatherless son.

Mindy and I had not planned any of this strategic placement. *But what could characterize this household more,* I thought, *than the joy God has given us after a horrible thing happened? We are full of joy, and it's God who has done it by sending Jesus.*

And then I thought of the familiar words of Jesus: "You are the light of the world—like a city on a mountain, glowing in the night for all to see. Don't hide your light under a basket! Instead, put it on a stand and let it shine for all. In the same way, let your good deeds shine out for all to see, so that everyone will praise your heavenly Father" (Matthew 5:14-16).

At the end of the long road of distress and pressure and upheaval lies the possibility of joy after all. We may not sense it at first, but God is at work behind the scenes. In time it will burst forth to warm our hearts and those of all who watch us.

18

Suddenly

If you get tired enough, your mind can start playing tricks on you. Once after a cold spell of days in the jungle, when our group was miserable and chilled to the bone, I got to fantasizing. It was the holy season of Ramadan, beginning in November that year, and the Muslims were in a bad mood due to daytime fasting. On top of that, we were in a place of heavy tree cover so that little sunshine got through, adding to the gloom.

And I thought, *What if here in the midst of the jungle we would stumble onto a real place to spend the night? A place with heat, and a double bed for Martin and me, in an enclosed room . . . clean sheets . . . screens on the windows to keep out the mosquitoes . . . an attached bathroom for us, with running water both hot and cold . . . fresh towels . . . a shower that works . . . a TV and phone.*

In the other part of the house a kind villager would be preparing a delicious meal of fried chicken with rice and gravy. And then when we retired for the night, there would be cookies and hot sweet tea waiting on the dresser.

It never happened that way. At least not until I

arrived at the U.S. embassy in Manila on the night of
June 7, 2002 . . . alone, with my leg in a splint.

The solution we crave when life spins out of control
can become vivid in our imaginations. If only this . . . if
only that. We know that God has performed dramatic
and sudden reversals for other people, and we yearn to be
added to his list. "In a moment of time, you could solve
all this," we pray. "Please, God. Just wave your mighty
hand and sweep me onto solid footing once again."

While our family was living in Aritao, before the
capture, we had a comfortable home. By American stan-
dards it was certainly plain—no air-conditioning, for
example, and no hot running water. But to our Filipino
neighbors in the barrio, we were doing well. Martin used
to remind the kids occasionally about 1 Timothy 6:7-8,
which says, "After all, we didn't bring anything with us
when we came into the world, and we certainly cannot
carry anything with us when we die. So if we have
enough food and clothing, let us be content."

He would continue: "Notice, it doesn't even mention
having a home. Just food and clothing. Are we content
with that?"

Now in the jungle, Martin and I had clothing (well, a
couple of outfits at most) and food at least some of the
time. The scriptural quota was ours. Could we be
content? Or would we go on pitying ourselves and wish-
ing for a Holiday Inn? We began to pray, "Lord, build
contentment into our lives, our spirits. Begin to change
us on the inside. We need to rest in your provision and
be thankful."

➵➵

One winter night after my return to Kansas, the kids and I went to see the Rose Hill High School drama department's rendition of *Joseph and the Amazing Technicolor Dreamcoat*. I've always loved musicals, and I knew some of the students on stage.

As you probably know, this is a funny and, at times, preposterous treatment of the Old Testament story of Joseph from the fertile mind of Andrew Lloyd Webber, who also gave us *Cats* and *Phantom of the Opera*. It uses all different styles of music. I laughed along with the rest when Pharaoh whipped off his royal robe at one point to reveal an Elvis Presley costume.

Amid the silliness, though, the hopelessness of Joseph also comes through. His brothers plot against him and sell him to a slave caravan. He winds up far from home in Egypt. There things go from bad to worse. His master's wife frames him as a sexual predator, landing him in jail. Fellow inmates promise to help him when they get out—but then they forget.

I identified with the feeling. I knew what it was like to be ignored . . . to think life can't get any worse, and still it does. As one song lyric says, "Joseph's luck was really out, his spirit and his fortune low. Alone he sat, alone he thought, of happy times he used to know."[13]

Then, within a matter of *one day*, Joseph's whole life turns around. He goes from prison to the halls of power at the imperial palace. Suddenly, everything is different. It's a lot more than luck at work. In the true account in

Genesis, God's hand reaches down and lifts the young man to unimaginable prominence.

I might have been the only person in the auditorium that evening who sat through the musical thinking about God's goodness! To me, it was all a portrayal of how you can be in a horrible situation, and then the very next day God can sweep you out of it. Sitting afterward in the van waiting for the parking lot to clear out, I said to the kids, "That play really had a point! It showed that you just don't know what God has for you around the corner. Things can look so bleak, but God promises there will be good if you love him."

Mindy gave me one of those "looks" a teenager flashes when she thinks her mom is nearing the edge. But I didn't mind.

Not all of us will be rescued as dramatically as Joseph, however. Yes, it happens, but not every time, and not according to any particular formula. I believe it is fine to ask God for a sudden upswing in our lives, so long as we do not resent him if he chooses otherwise.

I spent months in the jungle thinking and crying, "How long, O Lord?" Other believers throughout history have suffered even longer than I did. The mature attitude to which we should all aspire is that expressed by the apostle Paul from a Roman dungeon:

> *I want you to know, dear brothers and sisters, that*
> *everything that has happened to me here has helped to*

*spread the Good News. For everyone here, including
all the soldiers in the palace guard, knows that I am in
chains because of Christ. And because of my imprisonment, many of the Christians here have gained
confidence and become more bold in telling others
about Christ. . . .*

*I know that as you pray for me and as the Spirit of
Jesus Christ helps me, this will all turn out for my
deliverance.*

*For I live in eager expectation and hope that I will
never do anything that causes me shame, but that I
will always be bold for Christ, as I have been in the
past, and that my life will always honor Christ,
whether I live or I die. For to me, living is for Christ,
and dying is even better. Yet if I live, that means fruit-
ful service for Christ. I really don't know which is
better. I'm torn between two desires: Sometimes I
want to live, and sometimes I long to go and be with
Christ. That would be far better for me, but it is better
for you that I live.*   (Philippians 1:12-14, 19-24)

Paul is truly balanced between two options. Of course
he would love to keep living. But he also has one eye on
the heaven to come. Of course he would like to shake off
the chains and walk freely, resuming his apostolic travels.
But he is quite willing to stay right where he is and influ-
ence soldiers and visitors alike for Christ from his cell.

We hear no whining in his voice, no manipulation of
God, no pulling for sympathy from his readers. He is at
rest. He is content.

New Testament scholars believe that subsequent to writing this letter, Paul did get a release from imprisonment. His first letter to Timothy appears to have been written during this interim. But by the time we get to 2 Timothy, he is back in jail again, and he can sense the impending doom. His remaining days under the thumb of Rome will be few.

The exit from our current state of difficulty is impossible to forecast. It may come suddenly or gradually. It may take five minutes or five years. Meanwhile, we are called to stay faithful to the One who loves us and will see us through no matter what.

19

Not My Home

Nearly everyone in our society wonders what to say—
or not to say—to a widow. Do you mention the deceased
in normal conversation? Will she burst into tears? Are
you better off just to keep things light and upbeat? But is
that being respectful to what she is going through?

As you can tell by now, I talk about Martin all the
time. As far as I'm concerned, it's not a morbid topic in
the least. I often laugh at some of the great memories.
We had a great relationship, and I love recalling it. He
wasn't a perfect husband, but he was awfully close to it
in my book. I still love him and smile when I think of
him.

His sense of humor even shows on his gravestone.
Being a pilot, he was always irked that people would
assume a plane crash was probably the pilot's fault. He
used to joke to the kids and me, "I want you to put it
clearly on my tombstone: 'It wasn't pilot error!'" We
always had a good laugh about that.

Well . . . if you drive from Rose Hill about two miles
east on a gravel road to the country cemetery where
Martin is buried, you will see a tombstone that is a real
work of art. The engraver managed to create a lovely

177

tropical scene across the front, with mountains in the background, tall palm trees to the left and right, and a little plane coming in for a landing. The words say:

MARTIN RAY BURNHAM

Sept. 19, 1959 † June 7, 2002

And then if you walk around to the back of the marker, in small etching down near the grass it says:

"IT WASN'T PILOT ERROR." ☺ MRB

I love that! It shows the personality of a man who never took himself too seriously.

When I am around other people who have recently lost a loved one, I find myself out of step with the prevailing custom. Instead of saying, "Oh, I'm so sorry," I tend to say, "Oh, good—she [or he] is finally home! She'll never have to pack another suitcase or clean up another messy floor. No more good-byes, no more tears— she's home."

Well, at least that's what I *want* to say, because I truly have this big smile inside. I restrain myself if I feel I'll be misunderstood. But for me, the reality of heaven is so vivid now. I long to see it myself.

One of Martin's stock encouragements to me in the jungle, when he could see I was about to collapse, was "Just keep going, Gracia . . . who knows, tomorrow you may get to *go home*." Yes indeed! This world is not my home, as the old gospel song says. I'm interested in the real home above.

People still come up to me with sober faces, now more than two years later, and say, "I'm so sorry Martin died." I take their hand and thank them for their concern. But inside I'm thinking, *Well, yes, death is a rotten thing. But even worse would be to live a long life unhappily. I'm glad Martin lived a full and happy life, even if it was short.* I can't change who I am, and I can't be sad when I think about him enjoying heaven. I wouldn't wish him back here.

When you live in the Philippines, you learn a lot about Chinese culture, because many Chinese have immigrated to that country and done well in the business world. As a result, everybody is familiar with their calendar, knowing whether it's the Year of the Horse or the Year of the Dragon or whatever.

You also observe that the color to wear to a Chinese funeral is not black, but white. Why is this? They say white stands for happiness and prosperity in the next world.

Once when a Christian believer in our town passed away, the Filipinos said to each other, "Why should we wear black to the funeral? Our friend has gone to be with the Lord, whom he loved. Let's all wear white!"

They spread the word, and on the day of the service, there were white dresses and white *barongs* (dress shirts) everywhere. We loved it. The focus had been turned to the blessings of heaven that lay ahead.

People in the town who saw non-Chinese folks going

to a funeral in white naturally asked questions. This gave us an opportunity to explain that our friend was now in the presence of Jesus, who welcomes those who "will walk with me in white, for they are worthy. All who are victorious will be clothed in white" (Revelation 3:4-5). Nearly every description of an angel in the Bible mentions white clothing as well. What a resplendent scene awaits us in heaven! It is going to be gorgeous.

When we embrace the notion of heaven instead of fearing the transition that takes us there, it affects our whole emotional outlook. We open up in a new way to God's tender embrace not only then, but here and now. While we enjoy the earth and its pleasures, we're no longer satisfied simply with what this world offers. I was driving the other day when a song came on the Christian station that expressed the joy that comes from this outlook: "I am finally free," the song says. "My heart is spoken for."[14] I loved those lyrics, and tears welled up in my eyes as I thought about not only being God's child right now but also experiencing the coming joy of being with the Lord forever.

The concept of heaven as our real home also affects our practical outlook on daily living. A few miles north of Rose Hill is a working cattle ranch that also operates the Prairie Rose Chuckwagon Supper. After finishing a dinner of mouthwatering barbecue, guests are treated to a cowboy music show. A standing number on the Prairie Rose Wranglers' repertoire is the old country classic "I Am a Pilgrim and a Stranger." I often take guests there, and that song never fails to make me think. *Am I living as a pilgrim-in-transit now that I'm back in comfortable America?* I clearly had that view when I was stumbling around Basilan Island for a year with nothing more than a grimy backpack. Have I lost it now that life is easier? I hope not. I want nothing but to surrender my life, my belongings, my circumstances to the Lord, and to hold the "stuff" of my existence very, very loosely.

My Grandma Jones died not long ago at the age of 102. She was a gracious woman with a kind heart, and I have warm memories of going as a child to her home in Wynne, Arkansas, where there was always a big jar of pennies for the grandchildren to share. My brother and sisters and I would dump them out on the table and sort them into equal piles, then head for the nearby dime store to see what wonderful things we could buy. By the next time we visited her house, Grandma had somehow managed to refill the penny jar for our pleasure.

Now it was time for the funeral. We gathered from Kansas and Missouri and Indiana and Ohio and even Canada to honor this marvelous woman. My sister Nancy and I were asked to sing. We settled on the old Swedish melody "He the Pearly Gates Will Open," and soon our siblings were volunteering to sing with us, and then some of the great-grandchildren, and even my dad, until it turned into a little choir.

The song needed some kind of setup, I felt. I spent part of a morning contemplating this while listening to a CD about heaven. I came to settle upon a passage near the climax of John Bunyan's marvelous work, *The Pilgrim's Progress* (1678).

When we entered the funeral home that day, we stopped first to look at the many flower arrangements people had sent. Soon the pastor began the service with Scriptures of comfort. And then it was time for our song.

We gathered around the organ that Nancy would play, and I said, "Before we sing today, I want to share with you a passage from the famous classic by John Bunyan."

While they were thus drawing towards the Gate, behold a company of the heavenly host came out to meet them. . . . There came out also at this time to meet them several of the King's trumpeters, clothed in white and shining raiment, who with melodious noises and loud, made even the heavens to echo with their sound. These trumpeters saluted [the pilgrims] with ten thousand welcomes from the world: and this they did with shouting and sound of trumpet. . . .

Now when they were come up to the Gate, the pilgrims gave in unto them each man his certificate, which they had received in the beginning; those therefore were carried into the King, who when he had read them, said, "Where are the men?" to whom it was answered, "They are standing without the Gate." The King then commanded to open the Gate. . . .

Now I saw in my dream that these [pilgrims] went in at the Gate; and lo, as they entered they were transfigured, and they had raiment put on that shone like gold. . . . Then I heard in my dream, that all the bells in the City rang again for joy; and that it was said unto them, *"Enter ye into the joy of your Lord."*

Just as the gates were opened to let in the men, I looked in after them; and behold, the City shone like the sun, the streets also were paved with gold, and in them walked many [people] with crowns on their heads, palms in their hands, and golden harps to sing praises. . . .

When I had seen, I wished myself among them.[15]

So do I. I fervently wish myself to be among those who have been welcomed through the pearly gates to the Real World. There await Grandma Jones, and Martin, and so many others who mean the most to me . . . and to you. To join them once again will be the highest of pleasures for us all.

I never want to lose touch with the hope of that coming day.

20

It's Only Halftime

The world's largest boarding school for missionary children is Faith Academy in Manila. Perched on a steep hillside at the edge of the sprawling city, it offers kindergarten through high school for more than six hundred students whose parents are scattered all across Asia and the Pacific.

For decades, the basketball coach, Tine Hardeman, has been a campus favorite. He was there when Martin first arrived as a fifth grader, and only now is he thinking about retirement. A loving and optimistic man, he just has a way of pulling the best out of kids.

I got to hear him speak not long ago at an alumni gathering in Nashville. Of course he fascinated the crowd with basketball stories from over the years, and even though I never attended Faith Academy or played for him, I enjoyed the tales of glory and challenge along with the rest.

Tine's inspirational point was "You've got to *stay in the game!*" He talked about halftime, when the players troop off the court sweaty and tired. They glance at the scoreboard once more as they head for the locker room, where they gulp some water and slump down on the benches or the floor. The coach walks in behind them with much to say. He tells them what they've done well, but he spends more time on what they need to improve. He analyzes what the opponents have been doing and shows how to adjust. He winds up his pep talk with a rousing speech of "Awwright, let's get back out there and play a great second half!"

This became an analogy to our life. "Wherever you are in the world, and whatever you're doing," Tine said, "the game's not over yet. There's another half yet to go. My challenge to you today is this: *Stay in the game!* Keep pressing on, as Paul says in Philippians 3:14, 'to reach the end . . . and receive the prize for which God, through Christ Jesus, is calling us up to heaven.' "

I sat there thinking about my life. I wasn't an athlete, but I could still identify with his analogy. *It's halftime in my ball game,* I told myself. The first half was long. It went well for the most part. But the last two minutes were very hard. I lost my all-star teammate. I had to fight like everything to stay in the game.

Now—I've had my rest break. I've heard the halftime pep talk, I've gotten a cold drink, and the second half of my life is ready to begin.

To be honest, I don't even know what position I'll be playing, other than the position of mom to my three kids. Beyond that, I can't predict. Will I even have a public position out on the floor? Maybe I'll just be sitting on the bench cheering for the others. But the coach— the heavenly Coach—will let me know as the second half goes on. Whatever he asks, I will do it with all my heart. We want to win this thing! We want to dominate. We want to come out on top.

The day will come for me when the final buzzer sounds. But for now, there's a lot of work to do. A lot of running and passing and scrambling for the loose ball. My job is to give it every ounce of energy I've got.

It's only halftime.

Have you ever heard of Bert Elliot? Probably not. You're much more likely to recognize the name of his famous brother, Jim, who was martyred at the age of twenty-eight on an Ecuadorian river sandbar while trying to reach a primitive tribe for Christ. Four of Jim's colleagues died that same day in January 1956. The whole world heard their story of bravery and sacrifice.

Meanwhile, Bert Elliot and his wife, Colleen, never made a big splash. But they have played a much longer game. At the time of this writing, they have served the Lord in Peru (next door to Ecuador) for *fifty-three years*. They have established churches and have played a major role in founding the first Christian school in the country.

Who knows why some people's names become prominent, while others plod along doing what God asks of them day after day, year after year, with little earthly reward or recognition? These are heroes, too. And I have a feeling that heaven will someday balance out the popularity score.

The writer of the epistle to the Hebrews promises, "God is not unfair. He will not forget how hard you have worked for him and how you have shown your love to him by caring for other Christians, as you still do. Our great desire is that you will keep right on loving others *as long as life lasts,* in order to make certain that what you hope for will come true" (Hebrews 6:10-11, italics added).

At a certain point in the apostle John's vision of the future, he tells how:

> *The twenty-four elders sitting on their thrones before God fell on their faces and worshiped him. And they said,*
>> *"We give thanks to you, Lord God Almighty,*
>>> *the one who is and who always was,*
>> *for now you have assumed your great power*
>>> *and have begun to reign. . . .*
>> *It is time to judge the dead and reward your servants.*
>> *You will reward your prophets and your holy people,*
>> *all who fear your name, from the least to the greatest."*

(Revelation 11:16-18)

No matter what setbacks have come our way, we must stay in the game "as long as life lasts." The ultimate evaluation before the throne of God will deal with us all, "from the least to the greatest." The present is no time to quit. We dare not imagine that our effort in the second half will go unnoticed.

One of my favorite movies is *Apollo 13*, the dramatic story of the American-manned mission to the moon in 1970 that experienced an onboard explosion. The tension is nearly overwhelming as the Houston engineers work feverishly to try to get the three astronauts back to earth. At one point, somebody in the control center says, "This could be NASA's biggest disaster."

I love the next line from the flight controller, played by Ed Harris: "With all due respect, sir—this could be our finest hour."

And it was!

The present chaos in your life and mine is not the final score. We are still in the thick of life. With God's help, we can still salvage this game. We need to keep our heads about us, listen to the coaching, and play our hearts out.

Before I flew home from the Philippines to reunite with my children and rebuild my life, the American embassy was kind enough to arrange for a Secret Service escort team to make the trip with me. They kept a professional air, of course, as we flew from Manila to Tokyo to Minneapolis to Kansas City.

But not long afterward, I received an e-mail from one of the agents. He wanted to encourage me, and he did so by quoting the following lines from Martin Luther's famous hymn, "A Mighty Fortress Is Our God":

The body they may kill;
God's truth abideth still.
His kingdom is forever.

I have taped those words to my mirror at home. They remind me that as awful as Martin's death was, it was not the end of God's work in the world. And it did not have to be the end of my productive life, either. I intend to keep being a part of God's kingdom, which goes on forever.

THE END

(Well, at least I thought it was the end. It seemed like a nice, neat way to wrap up this book—until I made a trip with my children to Mississippi and had a talk with Reverend Hartman . . .)

21

*God's Best
Is Yet to Come*

The Mississippi trip was to visit a church that had long supported Martin and me during our Philippine work. The kids and I arrived on a Saturday, in time to have supper with Reverend Edward A. Hartman and his family. I didn't know them well, although we knew that this remarkable man and his first wife, Amy, were the parents of four little "stairstep" children when she began having headaches. She died about a year later of brain cancer.

I had been told that several months before Amy died, she stopped by the local florist and examined several prepared funeral arrangements. She frowned when she read the various cards attached because they were so depressing. She began thumbing through other cards on display, eventually pulling one out and laying it on the counter. "This is the one I want on my flowers," she announced.

Three months later, at her memorial service, all the flowers at the church and graveside bore the identical card: *Welcome to your new home.* Martin and I marveled at the strength of these two as they faced this trial in their lives.

Reverend Hartman is now remarried—a wonderful story that I won't take time to tell.

But my visit in this home was unique in two ways. First of all, this pastor knew what I had been through in losing a mate. Second, he took extra time to talk with me and encourage me. Normally when I go somewhere to speak in a church, I arrive a few minutes before the service begins, the pastor leads in a short prayer in his office, and I'm on! This was different.

After the meal, my kids and the Hartman kids headed off to a different part of the house, and we adults began to talk. The inevitable question arose: "How are you doing?"

I gave my stock reply: "Great. The kids are doing well. I'm doing fine. I think people must be praying for us because things are going so well."

Reverend Hartman then followed up by asking, "What are your plans?"

I hate that question. All I know to say is, well, I plan on raising my kids—and then??? I don't know. I came home from the Philippines to raise my kids, and then I'm done. I can die happy.

"No dreams for yourself?" he prodded.

"No, not really," I admitted. "I kind of feel like the best of life is over for me. I'll do the best I can as a single mom, and God will show me after that."

"Gracia," Reverend Hartman said, "that's not grace. Thinking the best is behind you, and you're just going to trudge through life from now on . . . that's all? Grace says, '"For I know the plans I have for you," says the

LORD. "They are plans for good and not for disaster, to give you a future and a hope"'" (Jeremiah 29:11). Right there from his armchair after Saturday night supper, this man preached me a little sermon, ever so gently. He explained the grace of almighty God and how that grace says the best is yet to come.

I listened that night with thirsty ears, if there is such a thing. I am sure that others had said something along these lines to me before. I even remember a scrapbook my little sister, Mary, made for me while I was in captivity to keep herself busy—an alternative to worrying and fretting. The last page said in big letters:

THE BEGINNING
(Most people probably think this is the end,
but they are wrong. I can't wait to see how
your new life turns out!)

This particular weekend, almost two years later, I heard those same words of encouragement from the right person at the right time—and something happened in my heart. I don't remember all the Scriptures the pastor used that night or exactly what he said, but just being in his home where I could see the grace of God so clearly made me want to listen and keep listening. Awhile later, we called the kids into the front room so we could pray together before the evening broke up. Reverend Hartman led us in prayer, asking for God to continue to grace us with his love and blessing.

I left Mississippi that weekend with a gift, a book he

had written back in 2001 entitled *Homeward Bound: Preparing Your Family for Eternity*. He inscribed it with a blue fountain pen:

To Gracia—The Best Is Yet to Come . . . Really!
EA Hartman Feb. 2004 Isaiah 40:11

Over the last few weeks, I have continued to mull over in my mind the idea of God's grace. Who says the very best for you and me has come and gone? Satan says that. He says the best for you is over. He says, "You are helplessly trapped in this bad marriage, and it can never be fixed." He says, "You don't deserve this illness. You'll just have to live with it and try to carry on till the end." He says, "You can't deal with these high demands that life is placing on you—why try?" He says, "Your child is totally out of control and it's all your fault—he/she will never amount to anything."

Grace, on the other hand, says, "No eye has seen, no ear has heard, and no mind has imagined what God has prepared for those who love him" (1 Corinthians 2:9). Grace says, "I will open the windows of heaven for you. I will pour out a blessing so great you won't have enough room to take it in! Try it! Let me prove it to you!" (Malachi 3:10).

I have so often fallen into the trap of thinking that I'm going through life making decisions, and God is constantly critiquing me. "That was a good move," he will say—or more often, "What did you do that for? You'll never get it, will you?" I never feel like I quite measure up.

As we study Scripture, though, we see a different picture. "Since God did not spare even his own Son but gave him up for us all, won't God, who gave us Christ, also give us everything else?" (Romans 8:32). "Do not be afraid or discouraged, for the LORD is the one who goes before you. He will be with you; he will neither fail you nor forsake you" (Deuteronomy 31:8).

Grace sets Christ walking along with us . . . a step ahead . . . leading the way . . . making sure everything that happens works together for our good and his glory.

Grace deals with those high demands in your life.

Grace makes that illness a shining triumph and grants peace as you go through it.

Grace says nothing is beyond repair.

Grace says, "The best is yet to come."

I'm not talking about eternity. Of course, heaven is the ultimate best. But what I'm talking about is here on this earth.

I'm not talking about a handsome, dashing man for me.

I'm not saying you will be rich or have a perfect family.

I'm not saying your illness will go away.

I'm saying we are children of the King. If we know God, "he has rescued us from the one who rules in the kingdom of darkness, and he has brought us into the Kingdom of his dear Son" (Colossians 1:13). All things are new. Our worth now is based on grace, not on our situation or our accomplishments or lack thereof. We can allow ourselves to be loved as creatures made in

God's image, though our body is broken, our thoughts confused, and our emotions troubled. And we can start to become hopeful that life can still be good—with a capital G.

That is where I stand today: trusting God to make something of me . . . to grace me again. Just like he graced me when he saved me. When he let me live with Martin for nineteen years. When he kept me going through the jungle for more than fifty-three weeks. When he gave me people like you to love and pray for me still. His grace never ends. It is here for each of us now.

FREE! Discussion Guide for *To Fly Again*
A discussion guide written by
Dean Merrill and Gracia Burnham
is available at no charge when you visit

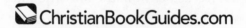

ChristianBookGuides.com

Notes

[1] J. J. Lynch, "Say Not, My Soul," quoted in *The Disciplines of Life*, by V. Raymond Edman (Minneapolis: World Wide Publications, 1948), 78.

[2] See http://www.caslon.com.au/dividesprofile6.htm for an interesting overview of the use of technology in the Third World.

[3] W. Phillip Keller, *Rabboni: Which Is to Say, Master* (Grand Rapids, Mich.: Kregel, 1997), 244.

[4] E. Stanley Jones, *Abundant Living* (Nashville: Abingdon, 1942), 74.

[5] *The Random House Dictionary of the English Language*, 1st ed., s.v. "worry."

[6] Henry Drummond with Harold J. Chadwick, *The Greatest Thing in the World . . . Love* (Gainesville, Fla.: Bridge-Logos, 1999), 26–27.

[7] Emily Elizabeth Steele Elliott wrote the hymn "Thou Didst Leave Thy Throne" in 1864.

[8] Jim Cymbala with Dean Merrill, *Fresh Wind, Fresh Fire* (Grand Rapids, Mich.: Zondervan, 1997), 19.

[9] Phill McHugh, "In Heaven's Eyes," © copyright 1985 River Oaks Music Co.

[10] Don Matzat, *Christ Esteem: Where the Search for Self-Esteem Ends* (Eugene, Ore.: Harvest House, 1990), 81–83.

[11] S. K. Hine, "How Great Thou Art," © copyright 1953. Assigned to MANNA MUSIC, INC., 35255 Brooten Road, Pacific City, OR 97135. Renewed 1981. All rights reserved.

[12] Annie Johnson Flint, "His" in *Annie Johnson Flint: Poems, Vol. 1* (Toronto: Evangelical Publishers, 1944), 135–136.

[13] Andrew Lloyd Webber and Tim Rice, "Go, Go, Go Joseph" © 1969 by The Really Useful Group Limited (PRS). All administrative rights for the U.S.A. and Canada controlled by Williamson Music Company (ASCAP). All rights reserved.

[14] MercyMe and Peter Kipley, "Spoken For," © copyright 2002 Simpleville Music (ASCAP) Songs from the Indigo Room Wordspring Music, Inc. (SESAC).

[15] John Bunyan, *Pilgrim's Progress* (London, Penguin Books, 1987), 139–141.

THE MARTIN & GRACIA BURNHAM FOUNDATION

*seeks to extend
the Good News of Jesus Christ
through its support of missions
around the world.*

GRACIA BURNHAM
Founder and Director
www.GraciaBurnham.org

*For more information on the variety of ways
in which you may donate to the foundation, please contact:*

THE MARTIN & GRACIA BURNHAM FOUNDATION

c/o Servant Christian Community Foundation
706 North Lindenwood Drive, Suite 100
Olathe, KS 66062
(816) 474-8800
www.servantchristian.com

The saga of the yearlong captivity of
Martin and Gracia Burnham
captured the world's attention.
People were amazed that they could endure such hardships
and even more that they could respond to their captors as they did.
What caused Martin to thank the guards
who chained him to a tree at night?

In the final days Martin and Gracia spent together
their thoughts focused on a passage of Scripture that says:
"Serve the Lord with gladness: come before His presence with singing."
(Psalm 100:2, KJV)
Martin said, "We might not leave this jungle alive,
but at least we can leave this world serving the Lord with *gladness*.
We can serve him right here where we are, and with *gladness*."

Such attitudes are not generated by human effort.
They are a direct result of the grace of God in the lives of his people.
It is this life-changing message that
the Martin & Gracia Burnham Foundation
seeks to share with the world.

The foundation's goal is to provide funding
for special needs in the areas of
missionary aviation, tribal mission work,
Christian ministries to Muslims, and
the often-neglected persecuted church around the world.

The horrendous ordeal is over for Martin and Gracia Burnham.
Though Martin is now with the Lord,
his message is far from being extinguished.
You can help continue the legacy of faith that Martin embraced
and extend the good news of the wonderful love, faithfulness,
and saving grace of Jesus Christ
to a world that desperately needs to know him.

What would you
do if you were
suddenly torn
from everything
you knew and
loved? When life
and death are on
the line, how can
faith, hope, and
love survive?

In the Presence of My Enemies
Hardcover: $12.97 (ISBN: 0-8423-8138-4)
Paperback: $7.99 (ISBN: 0-8423-6239-8)

In the Presence of My Enemies documents the whole
story of Martin and Gracia Burnham's year as hostages
among the Abu Sayyaf terrorists, where they faced near
starvation, constant fatigue, coldhearted murder—and
intense soul-searching about a God who sometimes seemed
to have forgotten them.

Whatever the struggles of your life, you'll find encouragement and hope in this refreshingly honest story of a yearlong battle with the darkness that inhabits the human
heart.